THE CAPTURED ECONOMY

THE CAPTURED ECONOMY

*How the Powerful Enrich Themselves,
Slow Down Growth, and
Increase Inequality*

BRINK LINDSEY AND
STEVEN M. TELES

OXFORD
UNIVERSITY PRESS

Oxford University Press is a department of the University of Oxford. It furthers the University's objective of excellence in research, scholarship, and education by publishing worldwide. Oxford is a registered trade mark of Oxford University Press in the UK and certain other countries.

Published in the United States of America by Oxford University Press
198 Madison Avenue, New York, NY 10016, United States of America.

Cataloging-in-Publication data is on file at the Library of Congress
ISBN 978–0–19–062776–8 (hardcover); 978–0–19–005900-2 (paperback)

CONTENTS

ACKNOWLEDGMENTS

Many people helped us to write this book. Here we want to single out a few of them for special thanks.

Steve would like to recognize Steven Rhoads, who first taught him to think like an economist (as well as when not to). Special thanks are due to the Kauffman Foundation, and Steve's program officer there, Dane Stangler, for their very generous support of the research on the rent-seeking society that went into this book. Steve would also like to thank Fawzia Ahmed, for a multi-decade conversation on inclusive growth (yes, we are in fact paying for inequality!), and for more recent discussions on the broader lessons of philanthropy and school reform. Mike Lind may not agree with much of what is in this book, but his support for Steve's writing on kludgeocracy is a major influence on this book's argument. Frank Baumgartner and Terry Moe will find their influence all over the arguments made here on how concentrated interests get their way in American politics. And Yuval Levin of *National Affairs* edited and published articles by Steve on kludgeocracy and upward redistribution that led to the writing of this book.

Brink would like to thank Peter Goettler and David Boaz at the Cato Institute for their support of this project. He is especially grateful for being allowed to spend much of the time he took to write this book in Thailand while waiting for his wife's visa application to be approved. He is indebted to his Cato colleagues Mark Calabria, Jeff Miron, and Peter VanDoren for reading various draft chapters and providing valuable feedback. Will Wilkinson and Ryan Avent also read parts of the manuscript and offered helpful insights. And Brink wants to thank his wife Meaw for her indispensable dual role as muse and refuge from the frustrations of writing.

Both of us want to thank David McBride of Oxford University Press, who was, as usual, as good an editor as any authors have a reason to hope for. We are grateful to Lee Drutman for allowing us to use parts of his article with Steve in *Washington Monthly*, and for his critical commentary on various drafts of the book. Finally, Dean Baker gets our sincere appreciation, not just for reading draft chapters, but for clearing the intellectual path for the argument we make in these pages.

RIGGED

WHEN AMERICANS THINK ABOUT WHAT it would mean to "make America great again," social mobility looms large. Back in 1970, 92 percent of 30-year-olds were making more money than their parents did at that age. By 2010, only 50 percent of 30-year-olds could still say the same. And looking ahead, only a third of Americans now believe that the next generation will be better off.[1]

Do these numbers mean that the American dream is dead? Perhaps not, but reports of its demise are not too greatly exaggerated. Because of a combination of slowing growth and rising inequality, the prospect of upward mobility and a brighter future is now receding out of reach for more and more of our fellow citizens. As a result, American democracy is weakening as well, as pessimism and frustration have smashed public trust in established institutions and opened the path to power for populist demagoguery.

The rise of income and wealth inequality, driven especially by rapid gains at the top, is one of the most widely discussed phenomena of recent economic life. Thomas Piketty and Emmanuel Saez have famously estimated that the share of total income accounted for by the top 1 percent of earners has doubled from 8 percent in 1979 to 18 percent in 2015—while the share of the top 0.1 percent has quadrupled from 2 percent to almost 8 percent over the same period.[2] Meanwhile, income gains for most Americans have been struggling just to keep pace with inflation.

Likewise, the dismal performance of the US economy since the financial crisis of 2007–09 has been painfully obvious to all. Normally, severe recessions beget rollicking recoveries, but not this time: the Great Recession, the worst downturn since the Great Depression, has been followed by the slowest recovery since World War II. As the malaise persists, evidence is accumulating that the growth slowdown reflects deep structural problems that predate the crisis.[3] Growth in real (i.e., inflation-adjusted) gross output per capita has averaged only 1 percent per year during the twenty-first century, half the average rate of growth over the course of the twentieth century.[4]

The combination of slowing growth and rising inequality has inflicted a double whammy on Americans' economic prospects. The growth slowdown means that expected progress in living standards has evaporated; high inequality means that just looking at GDP growth understates the magnitude of popular economic discontent, as the gains of growth have shifted away from ordinary Americans to benefit a relatively narrow elite.

The damage done by our economic malaise is not confined to the economic realm. The shocking election of Donald Trump—and the threat to liberal democratic norms and institutions that it entails—could only have happened in a country where confidence in the nation's leaders and governing institutions had sunk to dangerously low levels. And the failure of economic governance to deliver broadly shared prosperity is a major reason for that collapse in confidence.

There is a well-established link between economic downturns, such as we are now experiencing, and rising levels of intolerance, racism, and political extremism.[5] As Harvard economist Benjamin Friedman put it in *The Moral Consequences of*

Economic Growth, "The value of a rising standard of living lies not just in the concrete improvements it brings to how individuals live but in how it shapes the social, political and ultimately the moral character of a people."[6] When people feel economically insecure, they grow more defensive, less open and generous, and more suspicious of "the Other." When life seems like a zero-sum struggle, gains by other groups are interpreted as losses by one's own group.

Trump's supporters may have had relatively higher incomes, because they were overwhelmingly Republicans, and Republicans generally earn more than Democrats. But it is a low rate of growth, rather than a low level of income, that triggers authoritarian impulses. And Trump's strongest supporters—white men, especially those without college degrees—have experienced the slowest income growth in recent decades, lagging behind women, blacks, and Hispanics.[7] Even if Trump's supporters were relatively comfortable, they were concentrated in economically and socially distressed areas of the country.[8]

It should be no surprise that a demagogue like Donald Trump was able to exploit conditions like these. And the multiplying successes of illiberal parties and political movements in Europe suggests that the appeal of his brand of demagoguery might not be short-lived. So long as mainstream elements in the Republican and Democratic parties are unable to offer effective economic governance, voters will continue to be easily swayed by the siren song of populist authoritarianism.

The twin ills of slow growth and high inequality thus pose a serious threat, not only to our economic future, but to our political future as well. Although these problems are typically treated as separate and distinct, we will argue that they are driven in significant part by a common set of causes, with roots in the decay of our political institutions.

I INEFFICIENT AND UNEQUAL

The simultaneous occurrence of sluggish growth and spiraling inequality presents us with a paradox. The economic textbooks many of us read in school led us to believe that such a state of affairs wasn't possible. In what Arthur Okun famously called the "big tradeoff" between equity and efficiency, more of one always comes at the price of less of the other.[9] You can have faster growth if you are willing to put up with more unequal division of the rewards, or you can have a more egalitarian society if you are willing to settle for less dynamism. What we are not supposed to see is the situation we are currently living through.

Until recently, the prevailing explanation of economists for increasing inequality was rising returns to skills caused by information technology and globalization. In this account, inequality rises as a consequence of the expanded scope of the market, which is the engine of growth. Consequently, the only way to reduce inequality is to somehow equalize skills or else accept restraints on the market that would slow growth.

In the recent election, though, we witnessed the broad public embrace of a very different explanation of rising inequality— namely, that the powerful have rigged the economic game in their favor. Elites have conspired to hoard opportunity, manipulating the rules and their control of the political system to generate wealth for themselves, even as living standards for everyone else stagnate or decline. Both Bernie Sanders and Donald Trump owed the unexpected strength of their insurgent campaigns to the appeal of this classically populist message.

This folk theory of inequality should not be dismissed as the ranting of ignorant rubes. As with much popular wisdom, the specific mechanisms of elite self-enrichment that the public has latched onto—immigration and trade in the case of Trump supporters, campaign finance for supporters of Sanders—are not well chosen. This is not surprising, since crises of governance tend to delegitimize established sources of policy knowledge. The resulting vacuum leaves the public vulnerable to demagogues with superficially attractive and emotionally resonant alternatives.

But the folk theory is at least aiming in the right direction, a direction that more sophisticated observers have been slow to pursue. In real and consequential ways, the economic game *has* been rigged in favor of people at the top. As we shall argue in the chapters to come, across a number of sectors, the US economy has become less open to competition and more clogged by insider-protecting deals than it was just a few decades ago. Those deals make our economy less dynamic and innovative, leading to slower growth than would otherwise be the case. At the same time, they redistribute income and wealth upward to elites in a position to exploit the political system in their favor.

Economists and political scientists use the term "regulatory capture" to describe the dynamic whereby private industries co-opt governmental power for their own competitive benefit.[10] It is the growth of this insidious phenomenon that the folk theory has sensed. Capture of the policymaking process has produced a captured economy that serves the well-off at the expense of the general welfare.

Here then is the resolution of the paradox of slow growth combined with high inequality. Okun's trade-off between efficiency and equity no longer holds when the government is actively putting its thumb on the scale to favor the rich. This favoritism obviously exacerbates inequality, but its side effect is to reduce the competition and dynamism upon which economic growth depends. Accordingly, we now have the opportunity to kill two birds with one stone. If we can scale back regressive redistribution, we can enjoy more growth *and* a more equal society.

We do not dispute the accuracy of the conventional, market-based narrative of rising inequality—as far as it goes. The progress of information technology (IT) has indeed raised relative demand for highly skilled workers while steadily eliminating jobs in the middle of the skill spectrum. IT, combined with globalization, has given rise to winner-take-all markets with huge windfalls for economic superstars. Rising economic opportunities have created more wage dispersion among women, who have then tended to marry those of similar economic status, further exaggerating income differences between the highly skilled and everybody else. Declining employment in traditionally unionized industries has reduced the degree to which workers are able to demand a share of corporate profits. Meanwhile, the large influx of low-skilled immigrants over the past generation has widened the spread of the income distribution by swelling the ranks of those at the bottom.

Although the conventional narrative is a true story, it is not the whole truth—far from it. This book aims to tell the rest of the story. The missing narrative is that government has contributed actively to inequality, not just by failing to restrain naturally inegalitarian market forces but by distorting market forces in an inegalitarian direction. The rise of inequality is, to a significant extent, a function of state action rather than the invisible hand. And this state action, by suppressing and misdirecting entrepreneurship and competition, has rendered our economy less innovative and dynamic as well as less fair.

II BIPARTISAN BLIND SPOT

Recognition of this possibility has been slow in coming because of an ideological blind spot shared by left and right alike. The simple story that inequality is the natural result of unchecked market forces is very convenient to both worldviews. Those on the left use this story to argue that markets naturally generate morally unacceptable levels of inequality, while those on the right use it to justify inequality as a product of neutral rules.

This blind spot is revealed in fundamental contradictions that beset both sides' rhetoric. Many conservatives and libertarians have taken it as their mission to defend the distribution of income in capitalist societies.[11] Ironically, at the same time many of those same people criticize the enormous growth in government intervention and the resulting absence of serious competition in many sectors of the economy. But if it is true that the state has increasingly warped market competition, then that must show up in the distribution of income. It is no accident, we will argue later, that many of the richest Americans derived their wealth from sectors of the US economy where competition has been stifled and distorted. So conservatives and libertarians should not simply dismiss the subject of inequality as a function of envy or a hatred of free enterprise. They need to recognize that inequality is a threat to the political consensus in favor of market competition and dynamism.

Liberals and progressives have a mirror-image problem. Many on the left rail against unrestrained capitalism's innate and immoral tendency toward invidious inequality. Thomas Piketty caused a sensation with his book *Capital in the Twenty-First Century* by arguing at magisterial length that this tendency reflects the workings of a basic law of economics.[12] Because the rate of return on capital (allegedly) outstrips the rate of economic growth, increasing inequality is written into the DNA of capitalism, which means that only massive taxes and transfers are capable of reversing hyper-inequality. In Piketty's story, government matters only as the answer to inequality, never as a cause. It is also an article of faith among many progressives and liberals that, especially because of the role of money in politics, plutocracy exerts a strong and baleful influence over public policy. If plutocrats are indeed that powerful, does it really make sense that they would only use their power to produce neutral rules that in practice happen to favor the rich? Would it really not occur to them to push for rules that actively redistribute upward?

It is this bipartisan blind spot that helps explain the market for a huckster like Donald Trump. Unless we take steps to unrig our liberal democracy, we run a serious risk that the tide of authoritarian populism will extend itself, all the while entrenching the very crony capitalism that it purports to assault.

Market rigging by the already powerful is the primary mechanism by which high status is entrenched. While markets naturally produce unequal returns, they also have powerful mechanisms of creative destruction as well. When there are extraordinary returns by a particular firm, a market with low barriers to entry will encourage challengers to undercut incumbents, thereby driving down their rate of return. Challengers, or even the prospect of challenge, can force incumbents to invest their resources in innovation rather than accumulation, thereby driving economic growth. Competition is, in this way, essential to contain inequality as well as produce abundance.

Stunted competition is especially problematic, as wealth derived from distorted markets is recycled into influence over government. Incumbents can choose to invest in protecting themselves from competition rather than inventing new products and production methods or improving existing ones. Good political institutions are, therefore, absolutely essential to generating widely shared growth because they tend to minimize rent-seeking and force incumbent firms to fight it out in the market. As Mancur Olson famously argued in *The Rise and Decline of Nations*, and as economists like Daron Acemoglu and James Robinson have found more recently, when institutions are too weak to resist capture by the powerful and well organized, economic decline, corruption, and political instability grow in a vicious cycle. This is the cycle that has taken hold in the United States.

The good news is that this sort of decline is not inevitable. Liberal democracy is susceptible to exploitation by mobilized interests, as is any system of government. But it does have antibodies that guard against such exploitation. The problem we face today is not unlike the one faced by the country's founders over two centuries ago. As Madison put it in *Federalist* No. 51, "In framing a government which is to be administered by men over men, the great difficulty lies in this: you must first enable the government to control the governed; and in the next place oblige it to control itself." The modern version of that challenge is: how can we have a welfare and regulatory state strong enough to undergird a modern economy and render its outcomes tolerably fair while not using that power to simply transfer resources to the most powerful and best organized? Madison answered his question by observing that "experience has taught mankind the necessity of auxiliary precautions," by which he meant institutions designed to filter out the unruly passions and narrow interests of the populace so that governance can reflect a durable, broad-based public interest. We believe that, in our day, we need to develop and implement a new set of auxiliary precautions for an era with new threats to effective, popular government.

III DUCKING MADISON'S CHALLENGE

Neither the left nor the right has faced up to Madison's old but once again urgent question, much less come up with an adequate answer. In order to find a way out of our governing crisis, thought leaders and policymakers on both sides need to do better.

Conservatives and libertarians have failed by insisting that the baby be thrown out with the bath water. Once government assumes any responsibility to regulate in a given area, they argue, it is inevitable that rent-seeking will corrupt policymaking. Accordingly, the only way to solve the problem is to dramatically shrink the scope of the state. As the iconic conservative Barry Goldwater put it a half-century ago, "I have little interest in streamlining government or in making it more efficient, for I mean to reduce its size."[13] Contemporary conservatives adopt the same basic posture: The only way to get less rent-seeking is, in Grover Norquist's colorful phrase, to make government small enough that you can "drown it in the bathtub."[14]

This is a dead end. The modern welfare and regulatory state isn't going anywhere, and the reason is simple: the vast majority of Americans, conservatives and liberals alike, think it's a good idea. Although one of us wishes it were otherwise, there is no significant political support for a dramatic rollback of government's functions. Accordingly, the conservatives' prescription may sound bold, but really it is a counsel of despair and inaction: the problem at hand has only one solution, but it is impossible to implement.

This all-or-nothing attitude ignores the obvious fact that all governments are not created equal. There is enormous variation in the quality of governance across countries and here at home, across states and localities as well as federal agencies. Around the globe, bigger governments actually seem to do better in controlling corruption and clientelism than smaller ones.[15] Beating back rent-seeking here in the United States will sometimes require increasing the size of government; in particular, we will need to increase its analytical capacity and develop forms of government activity that cost taxpayers more up front but that are less susceptible to rent-seeking than those we have today.

Yes, rent-seeking is endemic to government, as all human institutions are flawed and subject to principal-agent problems.

But some nations—and some states and localities within this country—control those problems much better than others, and their example demonstrates that real improvement is possible. By casting all government as inherently incompetent and corrupt, conservatives enable the very incompetence and corruption they rail against. Disdain any efforts to make government more efficient and you should not be surprised if you end up with woefully inefficient government.

Analysts on the left, meanwhile, have grown increasingly sympathetic to the idea that the economic game is rigged in favor of the powerful. This has led them to shift their favored policy responses to inequality away from redistribution in favor of what is often called "predistribution"—rewriting the rules of the economic game with a specific view to altering the distribution of rewards.[16] In examining government as a source of inequality, these analysts on the left usually focus only on how the powerful use their influence over government to prevent regulation or redistribution. For instance, they have pointed to the decline in antitrust enforcement, financial regulation, legal encouragement of unionization, and taxation of high incomes as key explanations for the explosion of inequality. In one early and influential effort along these lines, Frank Levy and Peter Temin characterized these developments as a shift from the "Treaty of Detroit" to the "Washington Consensus."[17]

What this approach misses is the role of government action itself, rather than the government's mere failure to act, as a cause of inequality. Because of their attachment to the state as an instrument of social justice, those on the left have generally failed to recognize the egalitarian potential of constraints on government power. At least since the Progressive movement, liberals have favored liberating government at all levels, giving it the discretionary authority necessary to counteract business and regulate a complex modern economy. But an entirely discretionary government, operating through sweeping administrative power, is also a government that is highly susceptible to the influence of those capable of putting their claims before the state on an ongoing basis.[18] A liberated, discretionary government is also one ripe for exploitation by concentrated, wealthy interests.

IV TOWARD A MORE DELIBERATIVE POLITICS

Although the role of rent-seeking in slowing growth and accelerating inequality has been hidden in plain view for some time now, things are beginning to change. A small but growing list of influential thinkers on both the left and right have pierced the bipartisan blind spot and identified regulatory capture as a significant contributor to our current economic predicament. On the left, Nobel Prize–winning economist Joseph Stiglitz has sounded the alarm in a pair of recent books.[19] Jason Furman (writing while chairman of the Obama administration's Council of Economic Advisers) and Peter Orszag (former director of the Office of Management and Budget during the Obama administration) have called attention to the buildup of rents in a widely discussed paper.[20] Dean Baker of the Center for Economic and Policy Research has long been outspoken on the issue.[21] On the right, Luigi Zingales of the University of Chicago has been a prominent critic of "crony capitalism."[22] Under his leadership, the George F. Stigler Center for the Study of the Economy and the State pursues an active research program on the phenomenon of regulatory capture and its associated ills.[23]

What the analysis of upward redistribution has so far lacked is a plausible account of why high-end rent-seeking has increased so dramatically, and an agenda of plausible mechanisms for restraining it. In the pages to come we argue that this battle against upward redistribution requires a more competitive economy and a more deliberative politics. It requires combining the best of the two liberal traditions of the left and right into a liberalism that fuses both sides of a modernized Madisonian vision—a state strong enough to support a capitalist economy, but one made less susceptible to exploitation by the powerful.

At the root of our political economy problem is a failure of competition. As we will show in Chapter 2, the machinery of creative destruction is slowing down, the evidence of which is increasing corporate profits, declining new firm formation, and disturbingly increasing stability of the top firms over time. There is growing recognition of the connection between our sclerotic economy and increasing concentration of ownership, which has generated increasing monopoly rents. But competition is also essential for restraining inequality, by encouraging new firms to enter into the market and undercut or outperform incumbents with abnormally high profits. This has led many to point to the importance of increasing antitrust enforcement, which at the very least is addressing the right problem.[24] But an absence of competition also comes from the affirmative use of government power, such as when incumbents are able to fend off challenges by constructing barriers to entry like licenses or intellectual property protection.

There is no route to a competitive economy except through finding a way to a more deliberative politics. As we will argue in Chapter 7, rent-seeking is most successful when politics is least deliberative. Political deliberation is not a matter of being more genteel and polite. True political deliberation, in fact, requires political conflict.[25] Even a relatively small amount of conflict, generated by a modest amount of organization, can produce enough deliberation to eat away at the political power of the advantaged.[26] Only when both sides to an economic question are represented in the political sphere, and when the side of those who pay the costs of regressive regulation can force a dispute to the political surface, is true deliberation on the merits possible.

Deliberation also requires information, and information is costly. Someone has to produce it, whether it is the state or organized opponents of rent-seeking. A more deliberative politics places decision making where deliberation is most likely, and breaks open government when it has gotten in the habit of kowtowing to organized interests. Finally, deliberation is most likely to occur when the policies under consideration are relatively simple and easy to understand. When policies are complex it is easier to hide favors to organized interests, harder for opponents to hold politicians accountable for their actions, and more difficult for ordinary citizens to appreciate what is being argued about.[27]

This book is not a comprehensive analysis of everything that has gone wrong with America's political economy and how to fix it. What it does represent is an extensive set of economic diagnoses and political prescriptions for change that a liberal (Teles) and a libertarian (Lindsey) can agree on. In particular, we have both come to agree that in order to address the problem of upward redistribution and regressive regulation, a laundry list of policy reforms is far from sufficient. The right question is how to make larger political reforms that will reduce the ability of wealthy rent-seekers to get their way. If liberals and conservatives, for their own reasons and in their own ways, are not able to more effectively rent-proof our political system, the recent past will become prologue to an uglier future.

THE RENTS ARE TOO

DAMN HIGH

THE LAST FEW DECADES HAVE been a perplexing time in American economic life. Following a temporary spike during the Internet boom of the 1990s, rates of economic growth have been exceptionally sluggish. At the same time, incomes at the very top have exploded while those further down have stagnated. The wealthy, in other words, have been getting a much larger slice of a stagnating pie.

Economists have had an explanation for the latter trend, which is that returns to skills have increased dramatically, largely because of globalization and information technology. Roughly speaking, we have seen a large spike in the productivity of those at the top, who have been able to capture the value of their increasingly valuable skills. While deregulated and efficient markets are working, government has not increased the supply of skills through greater investment in education or reform in the organization of schools to match the demand for them.

There is clearly something to this explanation, but why should the more efficient operation of markets be accompanied by a decline in economic growth? Our answer is that increasing returns to skill and other market-based drivers of rising inequality are only part of the story. Yes, in some ways the US economy has certainly grown more open to the free play of market forces during the course of the past few decades. But in other ways, economic returns are now determined much more by success in the political arena and less by the forces of market competition. By suppressing and distorting markets, the proliferation of regulatory *rents* has also led to less wealth for everyone.

I WHAT IS RENT?

Economists use the term "rent" in a special way. For them, rent refers not to the monthly check you send your landlord but to the excess payment made to any factor of production (land, labor, or capital) due to scarcity. The technical and everyday uses of the word do overlap, since a portion of your check to the landlord does represent rent in the economist's sense. Specifically, when you lease an apartment in a desirable neighborhood, a part of your monthly check represents a windfall to the landlord that reflects the fixed supply of land in that location.

The scarcity that gives rise to rents can be natural, as with the case of land. Another natural source of scarcity is innovation: the introduction of a new product or a new, cost-saving production process. Once an innovation proves its success in the marketplace, it takes a while for competitors to match what is on offer or leapfrog ahead with something even better. In the meantime, the innovative firm reaps above-normal profits. These rents are only temporary, and they are self-liquidating: their very existence creates strong incentives for other businesses to whittle them away through competition. Moreover, these rents are dynamically efficient. The quest for temporary monopoly profits encourages innovation, and the efforts of business rivals to match the original innovator speeds the diffusion of good ideas and thus the growth of overall productivity.

But rents can also arise from artificial scarcity—in particular, government policies that confer special advantages on favored market participants.[1] Those advantages can take the form of subsidies or rules that impose extra burdens on both existing and potential competitors. The rents enjoyed through government favoritism not only misallocate resources in the short term but they also discourage dynamism and growth over the long term. Their existence encourages an ongoing negative-sum scramble for more favors instead of innovation and the diffusion of good ideas.

As a technical matter, rent is a morally neutral concept. Rents can reflect either natural or artificial scarcity, and their existence can be either good or bad for the economy. Nevertheless, the term "rent" is most commonly used in a moralized sense to refer specifically to bad rents. In particular, the expression "rent-seeking" refers to business activity that seeks to increase profits without creating anything of value through distortions to market processes, such as constraints on the entry of new firms.

Rent-seeking is nothing new. It is the ineradicable dark side of both market economies and democratic polities, and it has been there from the beginning. Writing at the dawn of the modern market economy, Adam Smith observed, "People of the same trade seldom meet together, even for merriment and diversion, but the conversation ends in a conspiracy against the public." And at the dawn of modern democracy, James Madison in *Federalist* Number 10 warned of the "dangerous vice" of "faction," or narrow interests opposed to the "permanent and aggregate interests of the community."

In both the economic and political realms, the prevalence of rent-seeking is a measure of institutionalized corruption. In the ideal market economy, the rules of the game are set so that the desire for private gain is channeled into bettering the lives of others. In the ideal democracy, the mechanisms of government are devised so that the clash of contending opinions and interests is converted into policies that serve the common good. To the extent that rent-seeking holds sway, the invisible hand of capitalism degenerates into the grasping hand of crony capitalism, and the lofty pursuit of the public interest devolves into a feeding frenzy of special interests. Free markets depend, paradoxically for some, on the existence of a state strong enough to enforce the rules of the game in an impartial, public-spirited fashion. Economic power must, somehow, be kept from being translated into the political power to game those rules for the benefit of market incumbents.

There is accumulating evidence that this degenerative disease of democratic capitalism has taken a turn for the worse in recent decades. A number of troubling indicators point to the conclusion that the American economy as a whole is becoming less competitive and less dynamic. While other factors may also be in play, this advancing sclerosis appears to reflect an upsurge in rent-creating policies that substitute entrenched privilege for the hurly-burly of marketplace rivalry. This policy-induced suppression and distortion of market competition is an important contributor to the two great economic maladies of the day: slowing growth and worsening inequality.

II WHERE THERE'S SMOKE...

Rents, whether good or bad, consist of above-normal market returns. Several concurrent trends indicate that, in fact, unusually high returns are on the rise. First, the overall profitability of US corporations has been climbing. Post-tax profits as a percentage of gross domestic product (GDP) bounce around quite a bit from year to year, but from a trough of 3 percent in the mid-1980s they have climbed above 11 percent as of 2013.[2] Some of this is due to increased profits earned overseas by

American companies, but it appears that the profitability of US operations is up significantly as well. While individual firms can earn gaudy profits temporarily in a competitive marketplace, an overall increase in profit levels nationwide suggests that something is amiss.

Second, even as total profits have risen, the distribution of those profits among companies has shifted. Jason Furman and Peter Orszag have examined the return on invested capital among publicly traded nonfinancial corporations, and they find that the increase in returns has been concentrated among the most profitable firms. While returns for the median firm have risen gently over the past thirty years, returns at the 90th percentile of profitability have skyrocketed: from under 30 percent in the mid-'80s to over 100 percent in the past few years.[3] In other words, during the same period when earnings inequality among individual workers has been on the rise, there has been a parallel increase in inequality among firms. The extremely high returns enjoyed by the most profitable firms suggest a big increase in rents, whether natural or artificial.

It is possible that the surging returns of the most profitable companies are due to a boom in innovation. Some of that is certainly going on: think of the high profit margins currently earned by innovative tech giants like Google and Facebook. But the rents from innovation are temporary, so if that is the main explanation, we should see brisk turnover in the ranks of the highly profitable. But according to Furman and Orszag, turnover has been quite low: 85 percent of firms with returns on invested capital above 25 percent in 2003 were still enjoying returns above 25 percent in 2013.[4]

Another indicator that points to an increase in rents is the recent rise in "Tobin's Q," or the ratio between a firm's overall market value (i.e., the value of its outstanding stock) and the replacement value of its tangible assets. For publicly listed US corporations, this ratio has increased about 20 percent since 1970.[5] Since a company's market value represents the estimated present value of the income stream from its assets, a rise in Tobin's Q means a rise in the value of intangible assets. Intangible assets can be benign in origin and may include a trusted brand name, intellectual capital that results from research and development (R&D) spending, organizational capital that results from an efficient structuring of production and management, or the human capital of key employees. But another source of intangible assets is government-created barriers to entry or special subsidies. The increase in Tobin's Q surely reflects the increasing relative importance of intangible productive assets in the post-industrial information economy, but it may also be a warning sign of an increase in rent-seeking.

Meanwhile, it appears that many US industries are growing increasingly concentrated. Between 1997 and 2012, the share of total industry revenue accounted for by the 50 biggest firms in that industry rose in three-fourths of the broad nonfarm business sectors tracked by the Census Bureau. More fine-grained analysis shows trends toward higher concentration in industries as diverse as banking, agribusiness, hospitals, wireless providers, and railroads.[6]

Does increasing concentration mean increasing rents? Maybe, though concentration can be measured in many ways, and there is no clear, stable relationship between any of those measures and the extent of meaningful competition. Accordingly, a shift toward fewer, bigger firms in an industry can mean greater dynamism and efficiency: think of the retailing sector, where the displacement of small, mom-and-pop stores by national big-box chains and Internet sales has brought huge gains for consumers. But it can also cause a slackening of competitive pressures, with higher prices for consumers and reduced incentives for innovation.

To the extent that industry consolidation creates bad rents, it's bad news for dynamism and growth, but that's a problem that falls outside the scope of this book's concern.[7] Our focus, after all, is on government policies that create rents in the form of entry barriers or subsidies. In the case of collusion or anticompetitive mergers, private market actors are driving events and the only government policy at issue is passive acquiescence.

So why talk about industry concentration in this chapter? The reason is that increasing concentration can be more than a cause of bad rents; it can also be a consequence of them. The creation of entry barriers makes it tougher for new entrants, thus reducing the number of firms contesting a given market. The awareness that potential competitors are unlikely to challenge an incumbent—that a market is not "contestable"—can make that dominant firm reduce the investment or innovation it would otherwise devote to preventing such competition.[8] In addition, the exploitation of special government favors can feature economies of scale. Seeking out cash cows made possible by government-created entry barriers and then milking them for all they're worth can require large-scale investments—like Washington offices for lobbying or large divisions devoted to tax avoidance—that make the optimal firm size larger than it would be in the presence of competition. When public policy subsidizes swollen firm size, whether directly or indirectly, you end up with fewer, bigger firms. So rising concentration is consistent with an increase in regulatory rents.

Another trend that suggests a rise in rent-seeking is the apparent decline of business dynamism over the past few decades. A buildup of entry barriers is likely to suppress entrepreneurship, while the prospect of political favors can divert entrepreneurship from innovation to rent extraction. Indeed, a host of economic indicators suggest that what Joseph Schumpeter called "creative destruction," the ongoing displacement of old firms and existing ways of doing things by new firms and new

ideas, is in a long-term slump. The rate of new business formation (calculated as the number of new businesses less than one
year old divided by the total number of firms) has fallen from
12 percent in the late 1980s to 8 percent as of 2010. The average
size of new firms has fallen (from 7.5 employees in the 1990s
to 4.9 as of 2010), as has the rate of employment growth for
firms that stay in business. As a result, the relative presence of
young firms (i.e., under five years old) in the economy has been
shrinking. The share of American workers employed at young
firms has dropped from nearly 19 percent in the late '80s to just
over 10 percent as of 2010.[9]

Some of the drop in the startup rate has a benign explanation. Much of the decline in the 1980s and '90s occurred in
retailing as big-box national chains grabbed market share from
small mom-and-pop establishments. This development gave a
significant boost to productivity growth and represented a triumph of entrepreneurial dynamism. On the other hand, after
2000, new business formation in the high-tech sector began
falling as well. High-growth young firms also became scarcer.
Compare firms at the 90th percentile of employment growth
with those at the 50th percentile and you'll see that the ratios for
both all firms and young firms have fallen substantially during
the twenty-first century.[10] In other words, the fastest-growing
firms aren't growing as fast as they used to.

All the trends cited above provide circumstantial evidence
of a rise in rents across the US economy. In other words, there's
plenty of smoke, but pinning down whether there is actually
a fire remains tricky. To determine definitively whether rising
corporate profits, widening inequality among firms, increasing values for Tobin's Q, growing market concentration, and
falling new business formation are the result of an increase in
government-created rents, we would need a good measure of
the size of those rents or the extent of rent-creating policies.
Alas, no good measure exists. The best we can do, so far at

least, is to identify crude but quantifiable proxies for the overall extent of regulation, and then assume that an increase in regulation generally means an increase in regulation-created rents.[11]

Some interesting work has been done recently with RegData, a newly devised index of regulatory restrictions created by researchers at George Mason University.[12] In the past, efforts to quantify regulatory activity relied on simple page counts from the *Federal Register* or Code of Federal Regulations—an obviously primitive methodology. RegData represents a modest step forward: it analyzes restrictive text strings from the Code of Federal Regulations (words like "shall," "must," "may not," "permitted," and "required") to estimate the extent of regulation overall and in specific industries.[13]

James Bessen of the Boston University School of Law has used RegData to test whether rising corporate profits and Tobin's Q values simply reflect greater investment in intangible productive assets (as measured by corporate spending on R&D, advertising, and "organizational capital") or instead are driven by rents. Bessen found that both intangible assets and regulation are strongly associated with the rise in corporate returns and valuations since 1970. But because investments in intangible assets have decreased relative to tangible assets since 2000, Bessen concludes that rents have accounted for much of the increase in profits and Tobin's Q values during the twenty-first century. Further, his statistical tests reject reverse causality, namely, that rising corporate returns and valuations are leading to increased regulation.[14]

In sum, recent trends sound a number of alarm bells that warn of a rise in rents across the US economy. Admittedly, the evidence is only suggestive: the circumstantial evidence admits of other possible explanations, and definitive quantification is beyond the current reach of social science. The imperfect measures we have, however, all point in the same direction—that such policies represent a serious and growing problem for the US economy. Even if government subsidies and entry barriers as a whole weren't getting worse—and the data strongly suggest they are—strong underlying trends toward both slower growth and greater inequality mean that we have less room for error where restraints on competition are concerned. To understand why, we need to understand exactly how rent-creating policies undermine growth and exaggerate inequality, and how those harmful consequences interact with deeper factors now shaping the pace and distribution of economic growth.

III STIFLING GROWTH

Modern growth theory, beginning with the pioneering work of Robert Solow and continuing with more recent "endogenous growth" models, makes clear that the ultimate source of economic growth is innovation: the development of new products and production methods that increase the level of output per given unit of capital and labor inputs.[15] Of course, the mere introduction of new products and methods is only the first step; innovation's full effect comes as the new products and methods diffuse throughout the economy. Introduction and diffusion together make for the dynamic process of creative destruction: new ideas originate and spread, old ways of doing things are displaced, and resources are reallocated from less to more productive combinations of capital and labor. Economists' best measure of this process is total factor productivity (TFP) growth, or growth in output per unit of capital and labor.

Regulatory rents do their main damage by interfering with creative destruction. By hampering the formation and growth of new businesses, they impede both the introduction of new products and production methods and the reallocation of resources that accompanies the diffusion of innovations. Recent research shows that both the birth and death of firms contribute significantly to overall productivity growth. According to analysis by University of Maryland economist John Haltiwanger, wide variations in productivity exist among firms in the same industry, and even among different establishments in the same firm. Moreover, these variations exhibit a clear pattern. Closing establishments are less productive than continuing establishments. New establishments, meanwhile, vary widely in productivity: those that fail quickly tend to exhibit low productivity whereas surviving new establishments are generally more productive than continuing establishments.[16]

Thus, the effect of "net entry" (entries minus exits)— otherwise known as creative destruction—is to raise the average level of productivity within an industry. Establishments with below-average productivity close and are replaced by above-average new establishments. Further research by Haltiwanger and colleagues demonstrates that this dynamic is a significant contributor to overall productivity growth. In manufacturing, they found that net entry directly accounted for approximately 25 percent of sector-wide TFP growth during 1977–87.[17] For retail trade, meanwhile, net entry accounted for virtually all labor productivity growth during 1987–97.[18] Here, the main engine of productivity growth was the replacement of single-unit firms (mom-and-pop retailers) by new establishments of national chains (e.g., Walmart). There are still many industries in the United States that suffer from rents produced by insufficient consolidation as a result of regulatory protection—everything from undertakers and optometrists to car dealers and realtors. That suggests there are still substantial productivity gains to be reaped by allowing national firms to compete with politically insulated mom and pops.

Besides net entry, aggregate productivity growth is driven by rising productivity within continuing firms and establishments, as well as changes in market share among those continuing units when more productive businesses grow at the expense of less productive rivals. Both of these other channels for productivity growth may also reflect the indirect impact of net entry, as competitive pressure from new firms stimulates existing enterprises to up their game.

Regulatory rents do harm not just by suppressing entrepreneurial energy but also by misdirecting it. The economist William Baumol speculates that a key variable influencing innovation and growth is how institutions allocate entrepreneurship between productive and unproductive activities.[19] If the policy environment is such that the best way to get rich is building a better mousetrap, entrepreneurial energy will be directed toward innovation; however, if it's easier to get rich by winning favors through the policymaking process, that energy will be diverted to negative-sum rent-seeking. Accordingly, a rise in rent-creating policies can lead to a drop-off in productive entrepreneurship.

There are thus good reasons to expect government-created entry barriers to depress economic performance, and the available evidence provides rich confirmation of that expectation. A number of cross-country studies[20] over the past couple of decades have found that policy barriers to entry, along with other restrictions on product market competition, reduce the growth of both overall GDP per capita[21] and TFP[22] in particular. Another study finds that product market regulation is associated with a reduction in innovative activity (as measured by the ratio of business R&D spending to output).[23] Others conclude that entry barriers and similar forms of regulation depress both total investment[24] and total employment.[25]

Even as evidence accumulates that rents are on the rise, it is also apparent that the US economy is becoming more vulnerable to rent-seeking's ill effects. Putting the state of public policy aside, the conditions for growth are now decidedly less favorable than they were in the twentieth century. In the past, even serious policy errors could often be taken in stride because the underlying momentum for growth was so strong. These days, however, the margin for error has shrunk. As a result, the US economy is likely to be saddled with subpar performance unless the quality of policymaking improves substantially.

To understand what's going on, let's break down measured economic growth into the constituent elements tracked by conventional growth accounting: (1) growth in labor participation, or annual hours worked per capita; (2) growth in labor quality, or the skill level of the workforce; (3) growth in capital deepening, or the amount of physical capital invested per worker; and (4) growth in so-called total factor productivity, or output per unit of quality-adjusted labor and capital.

Over the course of the twentieth century, these various components fluctuated in their contributions to overall growth. The fluctuations, however, tended to offset each other, so that the long-term trend line of growth overall remained stable. In the twenty-first century, however, this pattern of offsetting fluctuations has come to a halt as all growth components have fallen off simultaneously. Hours worked per capita surged from the mid-1960s until 2000, thanks to the entry of baby boomers into the workforce and rapidly rising labor force participation by women. Since 2000, however, hours worked have fallen as labor force participation has dropped sharply for both sexes. Meanwhile, growth in the skill level of the workforce has tapered off after decades of sharp increases in the average years of schooling completed. Net national investment (investment net of depreciation charges) as a percentage of net national product has been falling for decades, dragged down by the more widely reported drop in the national savings rate. And productivity growth, apart from an Internet-fueled surge from the mid-'90s to the mid-'00s, has been sluggish for decades.

None of this means that slow growth is inevitable from here on out, because the current trends are not set in stone.

Nevertheless, it is difficult to avoid the conclusion that the conditions for growth have deteriorated. Among other things, this means that the effects of bad policies are felt more keenly than before. Whether or not it is actually more virulent than before, rent-seeking now preys on a considerably weaker patient.

IV REDISTRIBUTING UPWARD

While regulatory rents are always bad for growth, their effect on the distribution of wealth and income is more ambiguous. When government policies create rents, the end result is always to redistribute income from groups with less political power to groups with more. This is true by definition: in this context, political power consists of the ability to win distributional struggles over fixed resources.

But although the rich and the powerful are often the same group of people, they don't have to be. Accordingly, regulation can redistribute downward as well as upward. The minimum wage, for instance, creates rents in the form of above-market wages for workers at the bottom of the pay scale. Likewise, collective bargaining under the Wagner Act confers a wage premium of roughly 15 percent for unionized workers. Overtime regulations, the Davis-Bacon Act mandating the payment of prevailing wages on public works projects, universal service requirements for telephone service and public utilities, rent control and tenant protection laws, and the Americans with Disabilities Act provide further examples of regulatory policies that create rents for the less-well-off.

Even when regulations limit or distort competition in favor of big corporations, the distributive consequences aren't always clear. Exactly how those rents are ultimately divided up among the corporations' workers, managers, shareholders, and customers depends on a complex interplay of factors. And when rent-creating policies conflict so that the victims of Policy X are the beneficiaries of Policy Y (hardly an unusual occurrence), the situation grows even more complicated and opaque.

Although regulations can redistribute downward and sideways as well as upward, there has been a clear shift toward more upward redistribution in recent decades. At the same time that other economic, social, and political developments have been widening the gap between rich and poor, regulatory policy has amplified those underlying inegalitarian trends.

Consider the situation in the middle decades of the twentieth century, when income inequality was falling. The post–New Deal economic order was rife with government-created rents, but they tended to redistribute downward or sideways. The minimum wage was relatively high and roughly three-quarters of the country's blue-collar workers belonged to unions. Strict immigration controls propped up wages of less-skilled native-born workers.

Policies to shield existing businesses from new entrants or price competition were endemic during this period. These included considerably higher import tariffs than at present, agricultural price supports, the Bell System monopoly, and price-and-entry controls in railroads, trucking, and airlines. But the distributional consequences of such anticompetitive policies were muddied by the fact that the industries receiving the rents tended to employ large numbers of semi-skilled, unionized workers. The Civil Aeronautics Board, for instance, certainly provided rents that shareholders and management could feast on, but they were shared with unionized flight attendants and aircraft technicians. Accordingly, even with policies that favored big business, some significant fraction of the gains was passed through to the working class in the form of higher pay.

Meanwhile, other factors besides regulatory policy were pushing in the direction of greater economic equality. Perhaps most important, rapid gains in educational attainment caused the relative supply of skilled workers to race ahead of relative demand, thereby shrinking skill premiums and compressing the income distribution. Another important influence was tax policy; not only did sky-high top rates redistribute income after the fact, but they also "predistributed" by sharply reducing incentives for businesses to engage in bidding wars for top talent.

Since the 1970s, by contrast, a whole host of developments unrelated to rent-seeking have united to widen pay and wealth gaps and to boost the economic returns that accrue to the very rich. Consider the wide range of factors implicated in the growing economic divide between the highly skilled (or, roughly speaking, the college educated) and everybody else. Skill-biased technological change, for instance, means that information technology serves as a valuable complement for skilled "knowledge workers" while substituting for less-skilled manual and clerical workers. The slowdown in the growth of workers' average years of schooling completed means that the relative supply of skilled workers lags behind relative demand. Mass immigration expands the ranks of low-skill workers even as demand for them has flagged. People increasingly marry within their social class, reducing the marital pathway to social mobility.

The factors contributing to outsized gains at the very top are similarly diverse. They include the rise of "winner-take-all" markets produced by information technology's network effects as well as globalization's expansion of relevant market size; a huge run-up in stock prices; continuing growth in the size of big corporations (which has helped to fuel rising CEO pay); and a big drop in the top income tax rate (which has facilitated the use of high compensation as a strategy for attracting top managers, professionals, and executives).

The changing nature of rent-creating policies has lent further momentum to this robust underlying trend toward greater inequality. Basically, rent-seeking has moved upmarket. Many of the downward-redistributing policies have been scrapped or severely weakened. The highly restrictive immigration quota system was abandoned in 1965. Private-sector unionism has been reduced to a small and declining rump of the workforce. The minimum wage declined steadily, both in real terms and in comparison to the median wage, although there is now a flurry of initiatives to hike it dramatically. At the same time, the old anticompetitive policies that sustained unionism even as they subsidized industry have likewise receded. Price and entry controls were eliminated in the late 1970s and early '80s while ongoing trade liberalization has steadily whittled away tariffs to almost nothing.

The main rent-creating policies that have emerged and grown in recent decades have a much tighter focus on help-ing out those at the top. As we will describe in the case studies that follow, sometimes these policies directly benefit higher-income individuals at the expense of everyone else. In other cases, rents are created for corporations in skill-intensive industries. Those corporate rents then translate into higher inequality among individuals in one of two ways: they are passed through either to shareholders in the form of higher stock prices or to workers in the form of higher pay. As to padded returns for shareholders, the regressive effect is fairly clear-cut—first, because lower-income Americans are unlikely to own stock; second, because tax policy subsidizes the pur-chase of stock by the wealthy; and third, because stock options have become a major element of compensation for high-value employees. As to inflated wages and salaries for workers, the industries in question disproportionately employ skilled workers and have directed the lion's share of pay increases to such workers. As a result, very few corporate rents leak out into the working class in comparison to how things worked in the prior century.

V THE TIP OF THE ICEBERG

In the next four chapters, we present case studies of regressive regulation: rent-creating policies that undermine growth while exacerbating inequality. The policies in question are (1) subsidies for financial institutions that lead to too much risk-taking in both borrowing and lending; (2) excessive monopoly privileges granted under copyright and patent law; (3) the protection of incumbent service providers under occupational licensing; and (4) artificial housing scarcity created by land-use regulation. The first two are federal policies, the third is administered primarily by states, and the fourth occurs largely at the local level.

With regard to finance, the rents we examine are created by subsidies, especially explicit and implicit guarantees of financial institution debts and policies that encouraged the growth of mortgage securitization. In the other three case studies, the rents are a result of entry barriers, whether in the economist's sense of barriers to market entry by new firms or in the literal sense of barriers to geographic entry. Copyright and patent laws and occupational licensing limit who can engage in particular kinds of commercial activity, and zoning regulations limit who can enter or do business within a designated geographic area.

Financial subsidies have been antigrowth in spectacular, cataclysmic fashion because they triggered a global financial crisis that destroyed trillions of dollars in wealth and caused massive dislocations. More quietly, all these policies continuously undermine economic growth by restricting vital inputs to innovation. The rents from financial subsidies divert large numbers of highly talented people from contributing to genuine innovation, luring them into highly remunerative but socially harmful regulatory arbitrage and speculation. Excessive copyright and patent protections restrict the recombination of ideas that is the essence of innovation by making some ideas artificially inaccessible. Occupational licensing hinders the formation of new businesses, which are frequently the vessels for new products or new production methods. And zoning puts artificial limits on urban density, a vital catalyst for the innovative recombination of ideas.

Meanwhile, all four of our case studies have similar distributional consequences; notably, all of them redistribute income and wealth to the well-off and privileged. Subsidies to the financial sector generate huge windfalls for a favored few while taxpayers are left holding the bag. Copyright and patent laws pinch consumers to fund fortunes in Hollywood and Silicon Valley and boost sky-high profits for Big Pharma. Occupational licensing inflates the earnings of protected incumbents by restricting supply, especially in higher-income professions. And zoning operates as a tax on renters and new buyers while stifling economic opportunity, all for the benefit of wealthy property owners.

Why focus on these four particular policy areas? First, we wanted to illustrate the diverse forms that rent-seeking takes. Our four case studies cover highly disparate subject matters, they are administered at different levels of government, and they feature widely varying forms of regulatory apparatus. Second, we wanted to focus on policies where the stakes are high. All four cases affect major sectors of the American economy. In all four cases, the antigrowth market distortions caused by public policy are large and growing worse. Further, the regressive distributional effects are relatively easy to trace.

Our four case studies by no means exhaust the topic of upward redistribution by rent-seeking. On the contrary, they are only the tip of the iceberg. High trade barriers and price supports for farm products disproportionately benefit large agribusiness. The Jones Act outlaws competition from foreign shipping companies in US waters while similar cabotage restrictions block foreign air carriers from US routes. Ethanol subsidies and the Export-Import Bank are just two of the more egregious examples of corporate welfare business subsidies larding up the federal budget. Government contractors enrich themselves at public expense with cushy cost-plus contracts. Regressive regulation at the state level shields businesses as diverse as auto dealers, funeral directors, and hospitals from competition.[26] We could go on and on.

Furthermore, it should be mentioned that even when regulations are aimed appropriately at addressing genuine market failures, they can still act as entry barriers—and thereby create rents—as an unfortunate side effect. Regulatory compliance typically entails fixed costs that don't vary with firm size, which means they give a competitive advantage to bigger, older firms that can spread those costs over much larger operations. While the possibility of incidental rent-creation isn't an argument against otherwise beneficial regulation, it does point to the need for careful policy design to ensure that harmful side effects are minimized. And the regulatory status quo exhibits clear signs that this need has not been adequately addressed.[27]

Our case studies, then, are meant to be illustrative rather than exhaustive. The problem of regressive regulatory rents is much bigger than these specific instances, but we hope that a close look at these instances will suffice to give a well-grounded appreciation of how widespread and serious the problem has become.

FINANCE

IN ANY SEARCH FOR POLICIES that slow growth and drive inequality, financial regulation is an obvious place to start. After all, the financial sector was Ground Zero for the worst economic crisis to hit this country since the Great Depression. As Harvard economists Carmen Reinhart and Kenneth Rogoff have documented, financial crises are terrible for growth because recoveries from them are generally slow and arduous.[1] The US experience since the bursting of the housing bubble certainly jibes with Reinhart and Rogoff's analysis, as the expansion in the aftermath of the Great Recession has been the slowest on record since World War II. According to the Federal Reserve Bank of Dallas, the total long-term cost of the financial crisis, including lost wealth and reduced output, exceeds 100 percent of current GDP.[2]

While the financial sector is prone to causing cataclysmic wealth destruction for the economy as a whole, it shows true virtuosity in bestowing riches on a favored few. Financial executives and professionals account for an estimated 14 percent of the much-discussed top 1 percent of earners and over 18 percent of the top 0.1 percent.[3] As to just how high compensation can climb, consider this eye-popping statistic: in 2004, the top 25 hedge fund managers earned more than all the CEOs of the S&P 500 *combined*.[4]

So if you want to understand how the US economy is producing big gains for those at the top and stagnation for everybody else, the financial sector is clearly a big piece of the puzzle. But a skeptical reader might ask if finance is really an example of government policies that restrict and distort market competition through entry barriers and subsidies. Or are the problems in the sector instead just a function of an *absence* of government action?

We think that in important ways the presence of state action is central to the problems in finance, but we recognize that many will be skeptical. After all, the story of the financial crisis is widely understood as a story of deregulation and free markets run amok. Can we really be arguing that the egregious excesses and blunders of the housing bubble are evidence that risk-taking by financial institutions was excessively restrained by regulators? The economist Brad DeLong, reading an article by one of us that anticipated the present book, took that to be the case, arguing, "Steve Teles's implicit claim that the rise of the financial plutocracy shows that we need *less* financial regulation seems to me to be completely wrong."[5]

This is not our argument. Our contention is not that the financial sector is overregulated but rather that it is misregulated. The existence of inherent market failures in the financial sector presents a strong theoretical case for prudential regulation to prevent systemic crises. In particular, the story of the housing bubble featured spectacular failures by private market participants, ranging from ignorance, arrogance, and incompetence to shady dealings and outright fraud.

That is not, however, the whole story. There have also been colossal failures in the public sector, and not just sins of omission. In this chapter, we will focus on the large and destabilizing subsidies that the government bestows on debt financing and mortgage lending. These subsidies are a major root cause of both the financial sector's excessive growth and its recurring instability. They are the source of massive rents for financial firms and a catalyst for the excessive risk-taking that misdirects capital and periodically convulses the larger economy. It is the existence of these subsidies, and their deleterious effects on both growth and the distribution of income, that makes finance an appropriate case study for our larger thesis.

Our focus here is highly selective. We do not attempt to identify all the rents that accrue throughout the financial sector, much less propose remedies for dealing with them. We make no pretense of offering any kind of comprehensive critique of financial regulation. We do not address the growing influence of finance on the rest of the economy, including the management of firms, which has had impacts on growth independent of system instability.[6] Finally, we have not tried to catalog all the factors that contributed to the most recent financial crisis. Our goal is simply to demonstrate that government subsidies to the financial sector do exist, that they encourage excessive risk-taking to the detriment of the country's long-term growth prospects, and that they create large, undeserved gains for financial executives and professionals. The state, in short, is implicated in the myriad problems with the financial sector not just through sins of omission, but also through sins of commission.

I THE MORTGAGE CREDIT EXPLOSION

Like many other advanced economies, the United States has experienced rapid growth of the finance sector relative to the rest of the economy, a process now widely known as financialization. Between 1980 and 2006, domestic credit to the private sector doubled from 94 percent of GDP to 198 percent, while the financial sector's share of GDP rose from 4.9 percent to 8.3 percent.[7] While these values dipped during the Great Recession, they have subsequently recovered.[8] Notwithstanding the crisis, financialization is still firmly in the saddle.

Much of the growth in the US financial sector's share of GDP has been due to growth in professional asset management, with fees rising in line with asset values. This aspect of financialization, then, has been a consequence of dramatic increase in stock market capitalization since 1980 and the growing dispersion of stock ownership through mutual funds and government-subsidized 401(k) plans. We will not concern ourselves here with this part of the story, except for acknowledging that it is a big part of the story and that it is partly traceable to state action.

The other big component of financialization has been an explosion in household credit, an explosion made possible by the financial innovation known as securitization. Between 1980 and 2007, total household credit soared from 48 percent of GDP to 99 percent, with the sharpest increases occurring during the housing bubble. Residential mortgages dominate household credit, which also includes credit cards, student loans, and other consumer borrowing. Over the course of this period, household credit extended by traditional banks held steady at around 40 percent of GDP. Accordingly, all of the relative growth in household credit was accounted for by the so-called shadow banking system, that complex web of institutions that pools loans and then issues securities backed by the streams of payments on those underlying loans.

The surge in mortgage credit and the expansive use of securitization were not purely market-driven phenomena. On the contrary, they were, to a considerable extent, artifacts of public policy. Large, complex, opaque subsidies for mortgage finance of one kind or another have been a prominent feature of American political economy for eight decades; securitization in particular took off in the 1980s after the previous conduit for channeling subsidies, the government-created savings-and-loan industry, ingloriously collapsed.

These subsidies do not look, at first blush, like upward redistribution. The ultimate intended beneficiaries, after all, are lower-income, would-be homebuyers who otherwise would not be able to afford a home of their own. The problem here lies not in the policy objective (even though we are skeptical that the usual rationales for encouraging homeownership really hold up under scrutiny) but rather the means chosen to accomplish that objective. Instead of subsidizing home ownership directly through transparent, on-budget fiscal transfers (such as matching funds for down payments up to a certain amount), policymakers elected instead to subsidize mortgage credit by bestowing special favors on the businesses that provide it. There are obvious political advantages to this path; notably, the costs are hidden, so democratic accountability for taxing some to help others is conveniently attenuated. But the economic costs involved in this choice of means—the costs of pretending to have a government smaller than it actually is—have been staggering, as have been the rents that accrued to financial firms that cashed in on the securitization boom.

The government's initial foray into subsidizing mortgage credit occurred during the Great Depression with various forms of assistance for the nascent savings-and-loan industry. Thrifts enjoyed special access to liquidity from the Federal Home Loan Bank Board and were allowed to pay higher interest on savings deposits than commercial banks. Furthermore, the Federal Housing Administration and later the Veterans Administration stepped in to guarantee mortgage loans, and by the 1950s, 40 percent of all such loans were covered by federal guarantees. Two new government agencies, the Federal National Mortgage Association ("Fannie Mae") and the Government National Mortgage Association ("Ginnie Mae"), were created to buy mortgage loans and thereby prop up a secondary market in mortgages. In 1968, Fannie Mae was spun off as a government-sponsored enterprise (GSE), and another GSE, the Federal Home Loan Mortgage Corporation ("Freddie Mac"), was established as a competitor. In short, savings-and-loans (S&Ls) were a deliberate creature of government policy, designed to convert short-term savings deposits into fixed, 30-year mortgages.

All went well enough until the 1970s, when inflation and rising nominal interest rates led depositors to flee banks and S&Ls because of the low ceiling on interest rates for deposits. Regulators responded by decontrolling interest rates, which left S&Ls paying high rates to depositors and continuing to receive low interest payments on those fixed, 30-year mortgages. By the early 1980s, the entire industry was basically insolvent. Regulatory forbearance, combined with misguided deregulation that allowed thrifts to deepen their losses by engaging in risky commercial real estate lending, succeeded only in greatly raising the cost to taxpayers when the industry was ultimately bailed out and liquidated in the late 1980s and early '90s. The total direct cost to taxpayers at the time exceeded $124 billion (not adjusted for inflation).[9]

Out of the ashes of the S&L industry came a new model for government involvement, securitization, led by the GSEs Fannie Mae and Freddie Mac. Ginnie Mae and the two GSEs developed preliminary forms of mortgage pass-through securities as early as 1970, but Fannie Mae's 1983 issuance of collateralized mortgage obligations marked the beginning of asset-backed securitization in its current form. Securitization looked to avoid the old problem of asset-liability mismatch that doomed the S&Ls. Now banks could originate loans and sell them to the GSEs for securitization rather than holding them on their books for decades. With the implicit federal guarantee of their debts, the GSEs were able to offer mortgage-backed securities that were considered as safe as government bonds, making them highly attractive to investors around the world. By spreading mortgage credit risk much more broadly, securitization promised to make mortgages, and home ownership, more affordable than ever before while reducing mortgage finance's exposure to booms and busts in local real estate markets. The icing on top was that the new securitization model offered a bonanza of fees and trading profits to financial firms—which suddenly had an entirely new asset class to play with—especially in the fast-growing "shadow banking" sector that emerged to cash in on this bonanza. Everybody wins! Or so the thinking went.

So why did things turn out so badly? The risk-spreading benefits of securitization are real, but a combination of political and market forces pushed the new system to become progressively overextended. Originally, securitization was limited to mortgages guaranteed by the Federal Housing Administration (FHA) or the Veterans Administration (VA), and other safe, high-quality loans. Indeed, the main concern expressed about mortgage-backed securities during the mid-1990s was the risk to such bonds posed by *prepayments* of mortgages by homeowners who wanted to refinance at lower rates. But Congress, looking at the huge profits the GSEs were raking in, decided that the implicit federal subsidy they were receiving should be employed to broader public benefit. Thus, the Federal Housing Enterprise and Soundness Act (generally known as the GSE Act) of 1992 directed the Department of Housing and Urban Development to set affordable housing goals for Fannie and Freddie. Initially, HUD required the GSEs to ensure that at least 30 percent of their mortgage purchases consisted of loans to low- and moderate-income borrowers. Over the course of the 1990s and 2000s, the target was then raised repeatedly, first to 40 percent, then to 50 percent, and then still higher.

Meanwhile, the market's apparently insatiable appetite for mortgage-backed securities led private label issuers without any government (quasi-) guarantee to jump into the securitization game. As of 2001, private label issuers still held only about 10 percent of the market; by 2006, their market share had jumped to almost 40 percent.[10] The place where the competitive field was most open was at the bottom of the market—namely, low-quality or "subprime" mortgages with high loan-to-value ratios (i.e., low down payments) and low or no documentation of borrower income.

The development of new financial products, a process once proudly called "financial innovation," further expanded the market for mortgage-backed securities and the demand for more underlying mortgages to be issued. In a beguiling bit of alchemy, low-quality mortgages could be transformed into AAA securities by slicing pools of mortgages into "tranches" so that the senior-most slices are the last to absorb any default losses. This alchemy could then be embellished with "synthetic" securities comprising tranches of tranches. Other derivatives, like credit default swaps, appeared to spread risk even more widely, fueling demand for even more expansion of mortgage credit.

Egged on by the combination of financial innovation and expectations of ever-rising home prices, mortgage lending exploded and underwriting standards collapsed. Charles Calomiris and Stephen Haber offer a good summary of that collapse: "In 1990 a mortgage applicant needed a 20 percent down payment, a good credit rating, and a stable, verifiable employment and income history in order to obtain a low-risk, 30-year fixed-rate mortgage, but by 2003 she could obtain a high-risk, negatively amortizing adjustable-rate mortgage by offering only a 3 percent down payment and simply stating her income and employment history, with no independent verification."[11] Rarities before the late 1990s, high-risk subprime and Alt-A mortgages went from 8 percent of new mortgage lending in 2001 to 36 percent in 2006.[12] For a while, the deterioration in credit standards kept the home price boom going, but eventually the bubble burst, nearly taking the global economy with it.

We recognize that there is an ongoing debate—infused with ideological enthusiasm on both sides—about how much to blame the GSEs and affordable housing policy, as opposed to good old-fashioned private-sector recklessness and greed, for inflating the housing bubble and thus causing the crisis that ensued. We have no interest in joining that debate, as there is more than enough blame to spread around. It is true that the GSEs were losing market share during the bubble years, and that default rates were higher for loans that were used in private-label securitization.[13] There is also evidence that the affordable housing mandates imposed by Housing and Urban Development (HUD) were not a major influence on the GSEs' purchasing decisions.[14] So a good case can be made that government policy was not directly responsible for the worst excesses of the bubble.

But that does not let the government off the hook. The mortgage-backed security industry was invented, developed, and nurtured by the government (through Ginnie Mae) and the quasi-public GSEs, and it was all but monopolized by them until relatively late in the game. Yes, private-sector actors eventually leaped in and added their own compounding follies, but they never would have been in a position to do so if public policy hadn't already laid the groundwork.

Furthermore, regulatory policy extended preferential treatment to securitization, strongly incentivizing financial firms to issue, trade, and hold more of them. Consider the Basel accords, which set capital adequacy standards for big international banks and served as the basis for US regulation more generally. "Basel I," announced in 1988, required banks to hold capital equal to at least 8 percent of "risk-weighted assets." Risk weighting substantially diluted the 8 percent requirement. While normal commercial loans were fully weighted at 100 percent, municipal bonds and residential mortgages received a 50 percent weighting, and AAA-rated securities (including mortgage-backed securities) were weighted at 20 percent. Not only were such watered-down requirements inadequate to control risk exposure, but risk weighting perversely exacerbated risks by incentivizing banks to concentrate their assets on mortgages and mortgage-backed securities.

Meanwhile, the extension of credit to progressively less-creditworthy borrowers that fed the securitization boom did not encounter any pushback from regulators. On the contrary, the rapid credit expansion of the bubble years was fully in line with the bipartisan consensus, pursued with equal vigor by both the Clinton and Bush administrations, in favor of encouraging homeownership by widening access to mortgage credit. Public policy may not have forced the private sector to engage in speculative excesses, but those excesses met with warm government approval at the time and were considered evidence of public policy's success. Finally, just as the speculative fever was about to break in 2007, the GSEs gained back much of their lost market share with big and spectacularly ill-timed purchases of low-quality mortgages. This late push made a terrible situation even worse.

The track record of US regulatory subsidies for mortgage credit is thus nothing short of abysmal. Instead of offering transparent, on-budget fiscal transfers, policymakers chose to promote homeownership by channeling subsidies through financial institutions, first with the savings-and-loan industry, next with securitization and shadow banking. Both of these models of mortgage finance, designed and propped up by public policy, ended in meltdown. Apart from the ruinous costs of financial crises, regulatory subsidies chronically misallocated resources by pushing financial institutions to direct resources toward household consumption (of housing) rather than productive business investment. In the end, all of this waste has been for naught. Prior to the securitization boom, the US home ownership rate had held steady at around 65 percent for decades. Beginning in the 1990s the rate started to climb, reaching nearly 70 percent by the early 2000s. The rise was illusory: the bubble in housing prices allowed the widening extension of credit to the uncreditworthy to look like a viable strategy for a few years, but it didn't last. As of 2016, after untold billions in losses, the homeownership rate had fallen below 63 percent, the lowest rate in 50 years.

Despite this record of failure, the government role in supporting mortgage securitization has only grown since the financial crisis. One might have thought that the subprime catastrophe would lead to a fundamental overhaul of mortgage finance, but that has not been the case. Instead, the old system has been propped up with the explicit backing of the federal government. When Fannie and Freddie went bust, they were placed in federal conservatorship, making the federal government the majority shareholder in both enterprises. Although this arrangement is supposed to be temporary, it has persisted for over eight years and shows no signs of changing. Private-label securitization collapsed when the bubble burst and never recovered, but Fannie, Freddie, and Ginnie Mae have kept on buying up and pooling mortgages and issuing government-guaranteed securities as if the crisis never happened. As a result, up to 80 percent of all new home mortgages are being securitized and backed by these state-owned enterprises as of 2016.[15]

II WE'RE FOREVER BLOWING BUBBLES

For all the arcane jargon and hyper-sophisticated financial engineering associated with it, at the bottom of the subprime fiasco was a very old and familiar phenomenon: an asset bubble.

Going back to tulip mania in the 1630s, asset bubbles have always been a feature of capitalism. Prices for some investment good start rising for whatever reason, which attracts other investors who want in on the action. At some point, the upswing in prices takes on a life of its own. Prices keep going up simply because people think they will, regardless of the underlying fundamentals. Eventually, something happens to pierce the collective delusion, the bubble pops, and prices come crashing down again. Alas, since rapid price increases based on fundamentals happen all the time, it's never clear that a bubble has occurred until after it's over—which is why people are fooled by them, again and again.

Asset bubbles are a glitch inherent in markets. Vernon Smith, the Nobel Prize–winning pioneer in experimental economics, has demonstrated this in a lab setting where groups of experimental subjects tasked with trading an asset will regularly inflate bubbles.[16] However, bubbles are more than a market failure; they are a human failure. The very same herd mentality that sweeps market participants into a speculative mania can extend to government regulators as well. This is what happened during the housing bubble. Regulators, by and large, were not sounding alarms during the boom; they shared financial firms' confidence in their risk management techniques and believed that the contingencies that could bring about a crisis were far too remote to worry about.

In a market economy with a healthy financial sector, the occasional bubble is therefore pretty much inevitable. What is most emphatically not inevitable is for a bubble to trigger a systemic financial crisis and a steep drop in economic output. For that to happen, policy errors of the first rank are necessary.

The US economy experienced another major speculative fever less than a decade before the subprime episode, the dotcom bubble. The collapsing stock prices of Internet companies produced a greater direct wealth loss than did the nationwide drop in home prices, but the bursting of the dot-com bubble occasioned no distress for the financial system and only a mild recession. Why the huge difference?

For one thing, the distribution of the losses was very different. Dot-com stocks were held mostly by comparatively rich people, so the losses fell on those best able to bear them; by contrast, falling home prices inflicted pain much more broadly. Furthermore, and crucial for our purposes, there was a difference in how the two bubbles were funded. The dot-com bubble was inflated with infusions of equity financing; the subprime bubble, on the other hand, was inflated with debt, not only mortgage debt held by home buyers but also short-term debt that provided the vast bulk of financing for banks and shadow banks alike. The evidence shows that debt-financed bubbles are much more damaging than those financed with equity, as the recessions that follow are much steeper and the ensuing recoveries are much slower.[17] First, debt financing by home buyers channels losses through the financial system rather than directly to households (as is the case with equity bubbles); second, heavy levels of debt by financial firms render them highly vulnerable to insolvency crises in the event of declines in the value of their assets.

Here we arrive at the root cause of the financial sector's fragility and a significant cause of its bloated size: its heavy dependence on debt, also known as leverage. Regulatory policy is a major contributor to this fragility, as large subsidies for leverage encourage recklessness and overreach by financial firms.

To understand the problem, it is first necessary to note just how strikingly unusual the financial sector's reliance on debt is compared to the rest of corporate America. For US nonfinancial corporations, a company's balance sheet is referred to as strong when the ratio of debts to assets is low. High levels of debt are generally considered troubling, a sign that an enterprise is struggling and in danger of bankruptcy. For most US companies, total outstanding debt amounts to less than 50 percent of assets, and for many companies, debt levels are appreciably lower.

For financial firms, the situation is radically different. Debt loads in excess of 90 percent of total assets are the norm, and debt-to-asset ratios as high as 97 or 98 percent are not unusual. This state of affairs has persisted long enough that people now take it for granted as somehow normal, but it wasn't always the case. Until the middle of the nineteenth century, debt levels for banks averaged 50 to 60 percent of assets; in the early decades of the twentieth century, debt-to-asset ratios of 75 percent were still typical.

Why do financial firms take on so much debt? They are drawn to the magic of leverage, or the capacity of debt to dramatically increase returns on successful investments. To take a simple example, let's imagine you buy one share of stock in Company A for $100 and sell it two weeks later for $110. Well done, you've made $10 and a 10 percent return on your investment. If instead you borrowed $900 to buy $1,000 of stock in Company A and then sold that two weeks later for $1,100, you can pay back your loan and pocket $100 in gains for a 100 percent return on your investment.

Alas, the flip side of these heightened rewards is heightened risk. This time, let's imagine you bought stock in Company A for $100 a share but now the stock price has fallen to $90 a share and you have to sell. If you bought one share with cash, you've lost $10 or 10 percent of your original investment. If, however, you borrowed $900 to buy $1,000 of stock, you're now wiped out. You can pay off your $900 loan but your original $100 is gone.

The funding structure of financial firms results in their fragility and instability. For a bank with a debt-to-assets ratio of 90 percent, a decline in the value of its assets (i.e., outstanding loans and other investments) of greater than 10 percent will render it insolvent. Since many of the bank's assets are illiquid loans whose present market value is uncertain, any perceived downturn in the value of a bank's assets will start to trigger concerns about insolvency, which could lead to liquidity problems as short-term creditors stop rolling over their loans. The bank will then be forced to sell off assets quickly, which likely means at a steep discount, further deepening fears about the quality of the bank's assets, leading more creditors to head for the exits, and prompting more fire-sale disposition of assets in a downward spiral. In short, financial firms' extreme reliance on debt makes them a house of cards that any stiff breeze can topple.

The precarious nature of the financial sector's funding structure is widely treated as normal, an unavoidable state of affairs that is inherent in the nature of financial institutions. Banks are said to engage in *maturity transformation* (i.e., they borrow short and lend long) and *liquidity transformation* (i.e., they fund their illiquid assets with liquid liabilities); accordingly, exposing themselves to the risk of runs by creditors is an essential part of what banks do. But there is no necessary reason why loans, by banks or anybody else, have to be funded by short-term liabilities. Institutions funded purely by equity, or funded by equity to a considerably greater extent than banks are today, are perfectly capable of making loans. In addition, there is a fundamental (though not always clear) distinction between liquidity risk and insolvency risk. A bank with much more equity funding than is the norm today, say equal to 30 percent of assets, would still face liquidity risk as its short-term liquid liabilities would usually far exceed its liquid assets. Yet, its insolvency risk would be much lower than that of a typical bank today because its relatively large equity cushion would allow it to weather a sizable downturn in the value of its assets.

The high-risk nature of the financial sector's funding structure and the extent to which the sector's borrowing habits diverge from the rest of corporate America are further obscured by the confusing, and sometimes downright deceptive, terms in which the regulation of banks' balance sheets is described. A bank's equity is referred to as "capital," and minimum equity levels set by regulators are called "capital requirements." These requirements (which as we will see are extremely lax and poorly designed) are frequently described as mandates that banks "set aside" a certain amount of capital "reserves," as if that money was being idled in a rainy day fund and not being put to productive use. This is certainly how banking lobbyists describe such regulations. As the head of the Financial Services Roundtable put it, "A dollar in capital is one less dollar working in the economy."[18] The impression left is that any reliance on equity funding by financial firms is stodgy conservatism that wastes opportunities for productive deployment of resources.

All of this is completely wrong. A bank's equity is not set aside, it is not a rainy day fund, and it can be loaned out or invested in precisely the same way as is done with borrowed money. Capital requirements are not to be confused with reserve requirements, in which a certain portion of a bank's assets must be held as reserves with the central bank or as vault cash. These requirements, designed as a buffer against liquidity concerns, really do tie up resources so that banks are able to meet depositors' demands for cash. Equity funding, by contrast, is fully available for productive use.

Indeed, Franco Modigliani and Merton Miller won Nobel Prizes for demonstrating that decisions to substitute equity funding for debt should have no effect on a firm's overall cost of capital, at least in the absence of distortions caused by taxation or other government policies (an important qualification, as we will soon see).[19] Since creditors have stronger claims to firms' resources than do shareholders, it is true that on average debt is cheaper than equity. In other words, creditors are more satisfied with a lower return than are equity investors. For each individual firm, the costs of debt and equity are contingent on that firm's debt load. The more debt a company has, the higher the return both new creditors and new equity investors will require; likewise, lower debt levels mean lower costs of both debt and equity. Accordingly, the higher cost of substituting relatively expensive equity for relatively cheap debt is offset by the reduction in the unit costs of both equity and debt that results from having a greater equity buffer against downside risk.

In light of the well-established Modigliani-Miller theorem, how do financial firms sustain such high levels of indebtedness? Given the general expectation that borrowing costs rise with increasing leverage, why are banks able to borrow so much without facing sky-high interest rates and onerous conditions? And why do banks stoutly resist higher capital requirements on the ground that equity funding is so much more expensive than debt?

First, financial firms may be able to rely more on debt because the assets they are borrowing against are much more stable in value than those of nonfinancial firms. As John Cochrane has pointed out, a diversified portfolio of loans and securities just isn't very risky, certainly not in comparison to the expected future profit flows of a single company.[20]

Second, beyond the difference in market fundamentals, financial firms' predilection for debt may also reflect a market failure. Specifically, in judging the trade-off between risk and reward when choosing how much debt to take on, financial firms may look only at their own individual situation and not take account of the destabilizing effects of aggregate leverage in the financial system.[21] Given the fact that banks borrow from each other and also considering the risk of contagion during bad times, levels of leverage that might be fine for a single institution become problematic if more widespread. This market failure may be exacerbated by compensation practices in the financial sector, in which return on equity is a major factor in determining executives' compensation. Executives therefore have a personal incentive to lever as much as possible, especially if the tail risks lie years down the road well after fat bonuses have already been paid.

Instead of correcting market failures that lead to excessive risk-taking, regulatory policy actually makes matters worse. Specifically, the government's efforts to reduce the harm caused when financial firms fail ends up subsidizing the heavy reliance on debt that makes firm failure more likely.

The main explicit subsidies consist of (1) the Federal Reserve System's discount window, established in 1913, through which the Fed can act as a "lender of last resort" and supply emergency liquidity to distressed banks; and (2) federal deposit insurance, first instituted in 1933, through which covered depositors are held harmless in the event of a bank failure. Both these policies are justified on the grounds of preventing and containing bank runs—a particularly serious problem in the United States because historical limits on branch banking rendered US banks under-diversified and consequently crisis-prone. Yet even as they reduced the risks of contagion and financial meltdown, these policies simultaneously reduced the risks of high leverage. Access to the discount window made banks less vulnerable to liquidity shocks and thus made it safer for them to borrow more. Deposit insurance, because it has never been priced in an actuarially sound manner, acts to subsidize heavy reliance on deposits to fund banking operations. Insured depositors are rationally indifferent to the financial soundness of the banks they patronize, as they will get their money no matter what. Accordingly, they do not demand higher interest rates from undercapitalized banks to compensate them for the risk of insolvency. It is no surprise, then, that the creation of a formal safety net for banks led to higher levels of indebtedness.[22]

In addition to these explicit subsidies, an implicit subsidy created by a string of ad hoc bailouts has further incentivized financial institutions to ramp up their leverage. Continental Illinois in 1984, the Latin American debt crisis of the 1980s, the peso crisis of 1994, the Asian financial crisis of 1997–98, Long Term Capital Management in 1998, and of course the financial crisis of 2007–09—again and again the US government has intervened with emergency assistance to prop up American financial institutions deemed too big or too important to fail. This implicit safety net has extended far beyond the traditional banks covered by deposit insurance to include investment banks, the GSEs Fannie Mae and Freddie Mac, hedge funds, money market mutual funds, and insurance companies. As a result, creditors of those financial institutions have been spared the consequences of their misplaced trust. Given the expectation that bailouts will again be forthcoming the next time a crisis hits, the riskiness of lending to highly leveraged institutions is much lower than it otherwise would be; thus, the interest rates that those institutions pay to their nominally uninsured creditors are kept artificially low.

The perverse incentives created by these leverage subsidies are known as "moral hazard," an expression that comes from the insurance industry to describe the reduced motivation to guard against risks that have been insured against. How moral hazard operates in the financial sector is widely misunderstood. The common picture is that if moral hazard is present, it must mean that financial sector executives are consciously making business decisions with an attitude of "heads I win, tails you lose." In other words, they deliberately make investments they know are risky because they understand that they will make big profits if the investments pay off, and if they don't, well that's the government's problem.

It's clear enough that such thinking is fairly uncommon. Yes, when a financial institution is already insolvent or close to it, executives may try "hail Mary" investments because they face no downside risk. Their equity stakes have already been wiped out so they are effectively making one-way bets. Such behavior was seen during the savings-and-loan crisis, as regulatory forbearance allowed thrifts with negative net worth to stay in business and attempt to recoup their losses with increasingly desperate gambles. This is precisely the pattern of behavior that Charles Keating notoriously engaged in back in the 1980s—and which the "Keating Five" senators helped to protect.

In the recent housing bubble, however, many of the most disastrous decisions were made by people with plenty to lose. Huge fortunes and sky-high incomes were on the line, and few could be complacent about the prospect of losing them. Far from seeing themselves as reckless, the unwitting architects of the financial crisis were highly confident that they were managing risks expertly and were shocked when the facts proved otherwise. Accordingly, it would seem that moral hazard wasn't a major factor in explaining what went wrong.

But in fact moral hazard was absolutely central to the story, and it is at the heart of why the financial sector remains a disaster waiting to happen. The main effect of moral hazard isn't on the incentives facing the executives of financial institutions. Rather, the main effect is on depositors and other creditors. Because their risk of loss has been artificially reduced by the formal and informal safety net created by government, they do not respond as normal market actors would to the heightened risk of insolvency created by extreme leverage. Because they do not bear the risk, they do not demand higher interest rates to compensate for that risk. Consequently, the normal dynamics described by Modigliani and Miller, in which greater reliance on debt increases the cost of additional debt and thus makes the cost of equity financing relatively more favorable, have been short-circuited or at least greatly attenuated. Financial institutions can keep piling up more and more debt without market consequences, with the result that those institutions and the financial system as a whole grow increasingly fragile and disaster-prone. Sooner or later, a relatively minor reversal of fortune will suffice to spell catastrophe because almost all margin for error has been eliminated.

The system as currently constituted is especially vulnerable to insidious, slow-fuse risks lurking in the tails of probability distributions. The economist Tyler Cowen has characterized the problem as a strategy of "going short on volatility"—in other words, "betting against big, unexpected moves in market prices."[23] This strategy can appear to work well for many years, as by definition the contingencies being bet against are rare events. During these good times investors earn above-average returns, amped up by leverage. Complacency sets in, as backward-looking risk management systems assure everyone that all is well. These systems, for all their mathematical sophistication, rest on a highly dubious and dangerous proposition, namely, that just because something never occurred in the relatively recent past for which data are available, it will never happen in the future. Eventually, a blue moon or a black swan appears in the sky, and all those highly leveraged bets now generate losses big enough to threaten the whole system with collapse.

III THE FAILURE TO LIMIT SUBSIDIES

If subsidies are a major reason for the financial sector's heavy dependence on debt, and if these high levels of leverage are the fundamental cause of the sector's vulnerability to crisis, isn't the obvious solution to get rid of the subsidies? Alas, if only the world were that simple. No matter how opposed to bailouts policymakers might be ex ante, in the throes of an actual crisis it is virtually impossible for policymakers to just stand by and allow big institutions, or lots of little institutions, to fail. The threat of contagion that leads to systemic collapse and economic meltdown is simply too plausible to ignore, so policymakers feel compelled to act, and acting means saving the failing institutions' creditors from the consequences of their folly. This conundrum is known as the problem of time-inconsistency: a credible commitment in advance not to bail out would lead to less risky behavior and thus no need for bailouts, but such a credible commitment is impossible because everybody knows that politicians will come to the rescue in a crisis.

Nobody likes ad hoc bailouts or defends them as good policy. The problem is that policymakers feel they have to do them when the need arises, which then makes it more likely the need will keep arising. With the formal core of the financial safety net, the Fed's discount window and deposit insurance, the situation is different. Here there is a plausible case that these policies are a necessary element of a well-functioning financial system, albeit one with unfortunate side effects. Even if banks are well capitalized enough to keep insolvency risk at bay, they are still subject to liquidity risk. At the heart of what banks traditionally do is converting short-term liquid liabilities (deposits) into longer-term illiquid assets (loans). They don't keep enough cash and other liquid assets on hand to pay all depositors at once, so if depositors make a mad rush to the exits, even otherwise healthy and profitable banks can be driven to ruin. The discount window and deposit insurance hold out the promise of reducing liquidity risk and, by assuring depositors they will get their money, eliminating the incentive to stage a run on the bank.

If leverage subsidies are difficult to eliminate directly, they can at least be contained—specifically by capital adequacy requirements. Such regulations, designed to ensure that banks have sufficient equity cushions, have long been on the books. Yet it is clear enough that existing rules have been inadequate. Indeed, in the run-up to the global financial crisis they actually exacerbated risks rather than reining them in. The fundamental flaw in regulatory approaches to date has been to assume that extreme levels of leverage are normal and necessary in the financial sector. Regulation, then, has been limited to tinkering around the edges, managing isolated risks created by a few exceptional cases while leaving systemic risks endemic to the whole sector unattended.

Eric Posner of the University of Chicago Law School has surveyed five different iterations of minimum capital regulation for US banks over the past 30 years, and he has found that none of those efforts was ever informed by any serious economic analysis of the pros and cons of different levels of minimum capital. Instead, regulators engaged in what Posner calls "norming," taking existing practice as the benchmark and then making "incremental change designed to weed out a handful of outlier banks." As Posner notes, "U.S. regulators took pains, even as late as 2013, to argue that their regulations would affect very few banks, only the bottom 5% or so."[24] Since, as we argue, it is the heavy reliance on debt by financial institutions across the board that is at the heart of the sector's fragility, that means that capital regulation as traditionally constituted has been limited to the proverbial rearranging of deck chairs.

Actually, capital adequacy regulation to date has been worse than inadequate; it has created new incentives for excessive risk-taking. As mentioned above, capital regulations based on the Basel accords employed risk weighting that created strong incentives for banks to load up their balance sheets with mortgages and mortgage-backed securities. Accordingly, capital regulations were a significant factor in fueling the securitization boom that ultimately ended in disaster.

If the dismal cycle of recurrent crises is ever to be ended, the norming approach to capital regulation will have to be abandoned in favor of something much bolder. There is widespread agreement among economists that higher capital requirements are called for and that the Dodd-Frank Act passed after the

2007–09 crisis, for all its mammoth size and labyrinthine complexity, did not come close to doing what is needed.[25]

There are many reform ideas in circulation, with varying degrees of departure from the status quo. Anat Admati of Stanford and Martin Hellwig of the Max Planck Institute propose straightforwardly that banks be required to hold equity equal to 20 to 30 percent of assets depending upon conditions.[26] Charles Calomiris of Columbia recommends an equity requirement equal to 10 percent of assets, and 15 percent of risk-weighted assets; in addition, he suggests that banks be required to fund another 10 percent of assets with contingent convertible debt that converts to equity when the market value of equity falls below 10 percent of the market value of assets.[27] John Cochrane of the Hoover Institution, meanwhile, goes all the way and embraces truly radical reform, arguing that banks should be funded 100 percent with equity. Any fixed-value liabilities of a financial institution must be backed by US treasuries; everything else must be floating value and equity-funded. To achieve that end, he suggests a tax on bank-issued short-term debt.[28] Cochrane's idea is hardly new; it is an update of Irving Fisher's "Chicago Plan" from the 1930s and in line with numerous "narrow banking" proposals made subsequently. Of particular interest, Fisher's proposal was endorsed back in 1995 by none other than Merton Miller of Miller-Modigliani fame.[29]

IV COSTS AND CONSEQUENCES OF SHRINKING THE FINANCIAL SECTOR

Lobbyists for Big Finance protest that reforms to reduce subsidies for leverage and mortgage credit would impose heavy costs on both the sector and the economy at large. They are half right. Without a doubt, blocking access to subsidized debt financing would raise the cost of capital for financial institutions. That is the whole point of higher capital requirements, to limit the destabilizing reliance on artificially cheap short-term debt. Likewise, removing subsidies for mortgage credit would mean fewer home loans; as a consequence, financial institutions would miss out on the higher returns that go with higher risk during the good times. Again, that is the whole point: reducing risk exposure so that, during bad times, the whole financial system doesn't come crashing down.

Where defenses of the status quo go wrong—spectacularly, extravagantly wrong—is in their assumption that what is good for Big Finance is good for the larger economy. It is true that eliminating or reducing access to subsidies would result in a smaller financial sector with lower apparent profits during good times. There is no sense pretending that reform would be pain-free. Downsizing the financial sector would result in wrenching changes for many people whose livelihoods depend on the current way of doing things. But the costs imposed on finance would be greatly outweighed by benefits to the real economy. The bottom line is that Big Finance has grown too big, and its excessive size and volatility are interfering with healthy economic development.

It is certainly true that financial sectors can be too small. This is frequently a problem, and a severe one at that, for less developed economies. Governments in those countries have often pursued a policy of "financial repression" in which the combination of interest rate controls and high inflation results in negative real interest rates. This is a convenient state of affairs for governments that run chronic budget deficits, but it stunts the development of financial intermediation since savers are stuck with returns below the rate of inflation. Thus, in the world's lowest-income countries, private bank lending averages a mere 11 percent of GDP, as opposed to 87 percent of GDP in the highest-income countries.[30] Meanwhile, corruption and spotty enforcement of contract rights hinder the growth of capital markets. This is why family-owned conglomerates are so common in poorer countries. When blood ties are more trustworthy than the legal system, the former must serve as the primary nexus for allocating capital.

The prevalence of stunted, underdeveloped financial sectors around the world explains why, at the global level, there is a strong positive association between the size of a country's financial sector and both the size and growth rate of its overall economy.[31] Healthy financial development promotes healthy economic development in two basic ways. First, the growth of financial intermediation means more household savings get mobilized for productive use instead of sitting idle under the proverbial mattress. Second, banks and capital markets are generally better able to identify which individuals and businesses should receive financing than are the alternative mechanisms for allocating capital, namely, government, on the one hand, and informal networks of families and friends, on the other.

So yes, the financial sector can be too small. It doesn't follow that it can never be too big. Recent studies by economists at the International Monetary Fund (IMF) and the Bank of International Settlements (BIS) marshal evidence that the relationship between financial development and economic growth is inverted-U-shaped; in other words, positive up to a certain point but then negative thereafter.[32] They estimate that the turning point is reached when total private credit is around 100 percent of GDP; beyond that point, further financial deepening starts to constitute a drag on growth. As to the United States, private credit approached 200 percent of GDP in the years before the 2007–09 crisis.

In addition, the BIS economists show that faster financial sector growth is associated with lower productivity growth. They compare a country in which the financial sector's share of total employment is stable to one experiencing an average-sized financial boom (in which relative financial sector employment grows 1.6 percentage points per year), and they find that the former country's productivity growth is 0.5 percentage points higher, a sizable advantage given that productivity growth averaged 1.3 percent per year in their sample.[33]

Why is too much finance bad for growth? There are two main possibilities. First, excessive growth in credit can fuel instability that erupts in a financial crisis. Sound familiar? According to research by William Easterly, Roumeen Islam, and Joseph E. Stiglitz, the relationship between financial sector size and macroeconomic volatility also exhibits an inverted-U-shaped pattern. Up to a certain point, growth of the financial sector has a calming effect on the economy, buffering shocks and ensuring stability. Past that point, continued growth leads to a buildup of risks and greater volatility in growth.[34] And as economists Gary and Valerie Ramey have documented, countries with more volatile growth rates also have lower rates of growth over the longer term.[35]

Second, financialization can undermine growth through the chronic misallocation of resources. The financial sector extends credit to businesses to fund their operations and investments, and to households to fund their consumption. The positive association between financial development and growth turns entirely on growth of credit to the business sector; there is no known connection between expanded household credit and faster growth.[36] Indeed, there is evidence that more credit to the household sector reduces savings rates with negative implications for growth.[37] Accordingly, to the extent that a larger financial sector focuses more on household credit, it may be diverting resources away from productive activities. Even if we just focus on finance for the enterprise sector, more financial intermediation disproportionately benefits sectors of the economy where collateral is relatively favorable but productivity growth is low, such as in construction.[38] By contrast, enterprises with the most growth potential these days are generally built on human and intellectual capital, assets that cannot be pledged as collateral. Here again, more financial intermediation may end up with more resources diverted to relatively unproductive activities.

In addition, the financial sector is skilled labor–intensive, meaning its workforce is disproportionately highly educated and highly skilled. Accordingly, a financial boom can soak up talented workers who might otherwise be engineers, entrepreneurs, or elite civil servants or social entrepreneurs. Note that in 2008, on the eve of the crisis, 28 percent of new Harvard graduates took jobs in finance, up from only 6 percent in the period 1969–73.[39] This is yet another way in which financialization can misdirect valuable resources to the detriment of long-term growth prospects.

It's no puzzle why the best and brightest have flocked to jobs in finance. With the progress of financialization, pay scales for financial services have raced ahead of those for other industries. In 1980, comparably skilled workers in finance and other sectors earned about the same, but by 2006 jobs in financial services were paying 50 percent more on average, and top executives were earning a 250 percent premium.[40] Amy Binder has also shown that financial firms are able to use their extraordinary profits to deeply shape college students' perception of what occupations are "prestigious," by acting as a constant presence on campus. Students enter elite universities with very little consciousness of finance as a career destination, but by the time they graduate they have been carefully groomed to think of jobs in finance as the most desirable option.[41]

There are market-based reasons for rising compensation in the financial sector. In particular, with the development of increasingly sophisticated financial products, jobs in the sector are considerably more skill-intensive than in prior decades. Furthermore, the huge increase in asset values has produced a windfall for everyone receiving fees based on the dollar values being traded.

In addition, an important part of the story has been the pass-through of rents. Subsidies to leverage and mortgage credit heightened apparent profits during good times, and compensation schemes throughout the financial sector were tied to return on equity.[42] When the illusory nature of much of those profits was eventually revealed during the crash, executives and professionals had already banked many years of fat bonuses. In this way, rents in the financial sector have made a significant contribution to rising high-end income and wealth inequality.

Reducing the rents from regulatory subsidies would not unwind all of the financialization of recent decades, but the effects would be significant. A less-subsidized financial sector would be a smaller financial sector, and a healthier one. A smaller, healthier financial sector, meanwhile, would mean a larger, healthier real economy, an economy no longer convulsed by periodic financial crises, and one in which the focus of innovation is on new products and production methods rather than circumventing regulation. Although the country's most talented young workers would no longer have as many opportunities to earn lavish riches in finance, the bright side is that they would face improved incentives to make valuable contributions to the nation's economic future rather than robbing from it.

INTELLECTUAL PROPERTY

IN OUR ROGUES' GALLERY OF case studies, copyright and patent laws are the wolves in sheep's clothing. According to the ingenious and highly effective rhetoric of their beneficiaries and supporters, these laws are the very antithesis of rent-seeking. Far from conferring special and undeserved privileges, they merely defend rightful property owners, owners of intellectual property (IP), from "theft" and "piracy." While rent-seeking misallocates resources and retards growth, intellectual property advocates claim that patent and copyright protections unleash artistic creativity and technological innovation by securing for artists and inventors just recompense for their efforts. Copyright and patent laws, therefore, are not only an integral part of the private property system that undergirds all market economies, but they are also a vital linchpin of innovation and growth in the contemporary knowledge-based economy.

In the United States, legal protections for intellectual property trace back to the Constitution, and the spread of such protections worldwide has now made them a pervasive element of the global market economy. Just as their supporters claim, intellectual property protection does deliver real benefits. By preventing others from copying their work, at least temporarily, IP protection boosts the payoff for artists and inventors and thus gives them stronger incentives to create and innovate. The problem is that IP protection also imposes costs, not just on consumers who have to pay higher prices for copyrighted and patented goods, but also on other artists and innovators. Unfortunately, a radical and ill-considered expansion in the scope and reach of this protection over the past few decades has resulted in a dramatic escalation of those costs with little in the way of compensating benefits. As a result, the rents that now accrue to movie studios, record companies, software producers, pharmaceutical firms, and other IP holders amount to a significant drag on innovation and growth, the very opposite of IP law's stated purpose. To understand why, we first need to understand just how transformative the recent expansions of copyright and patent protection have been.

I THE SILENT IP REVOLUTION

For much of American history, US copyright law was quite narrow and modest, especially in comparison to continental Europe. Translations and even abridgments weren't considered infringements in the early days of copyright, and foreign authors weren't granted copyright protection until 1891.

As the United States transformed from a cultural importer to a major cultural exporter over the course of the twentieth century, the constellation of political pressures acting on Congress changed, and the law changed with it, moving in a decidedly European direction. Beginning with the Copyright Act of 1976, the system of copyright "formalities" was progressively dismantled. Formerly, authors had to register with the copyright office and place a copyright notice on their works in order to enjoy the law's protection; now those requirements are no longer in effect. That same 1976 law extended copyright protection to unpublished works. These two changes massively expanded the scope of works subject to copyright protection. So, too, did the steady lengthening of copyright terms.

Originally set at 14 years with the possibility of one 14-year renewal, copyright terms lengthened to 28 years with a 28-year renewal before passage of the 1976 law. That law further extended terms to life of the author plus 50 years. The Sonny Bono Copyright Extension Act of 1998 pumped them up yet again, to life plus 70 years.

The instrumentalities by which copyrights are enforced have also escalated greatly in both range and severity. Traditionally, legal exposure from copyright infringement meant vulnerability to civil lawsuits filed by aggrieved private individuals or firms. Increasingly, copyright enforcement takes the form of criminal prosecutions by the federal government. Penalties have been stiffened dramatically, with the maximum fine per infringement soaring from $1,000 in 1975 to $250,000 today, and the maximum prison term rising from one year to five years. Since the Pro-IP Act of 2008, the federal government has stepped up use of civil asset forfeiture in its enforcement actions, seizing website domains allegedly used by copyright infringers and freezing defendants' funds. These hardball tactics create a chilling effect because defendants are intimidated into settling rather than face jail time and expropriation. As a result, the practical boundaries of copyright protection are defined by the zeal of prosecutors rather than by the interpretive judgments of courts.

The anti-circumvention provisions of the Digital Millennium Copyright Act (DMCA) of 1998 took matters a step further by effectively deputizing copyright holders themselves to set the limits of the law. The DMCA makes it illegal to manufacture or sell any tool or technology that allows users to bypass access or use controls on digital goods installed by their makers; furthermore, it outlaws (with limited exceptions) acts by companies or private individuals to defeat such controls. This is why you are unable to download a DVD for playback on another device in the same way you can rip a CD. If you figure out how to get around the encryption software on the DVD, you are committing a federal crime. For the purposes of this law, it doesn't matter that the use of the copyrighted material once accessed is permissible (e.g., because it constitutes "fair use"). Accordingly, the effective scope of the fair use doctrine, an important check on the perverse consequences of expanding copyright restrictions to encompass derivative works, has been reduced for digital goods by allowing copyright holders to decide how consumers can use the products they buy.

With regard to patents, the expansion of the law during recent decades has occurred largely through court decisions rather than via new legislation. In 1982, the newly established Court of Appeals for the Federal Circuit (CAFC) was vested with exclusive appellate jurisdiction over patent cases. Since then, the CAFC has reshaped the law by lowering the standards for patentability and expanding the scope of patentable inventions to include software, business methods, and even parts of the human genome. As a result, the number of patents issued annually by the US Patent and Trademark Office has increased almost fivefold, from 61,620 in 1983 to 109,414 10 years later, to 186,591 another decade later, to 302,150 in 2013.[1]

Until the 1970s, intellectual property was a sleepy little backwater of American law. The benefits of IP protection may have been modest, but so were the costs. Since then, the scale and complexity of IP law have exploded even as, with the rise of the information economy, the relative importance of IP-intensive industries has soared. From entertainment to software to pharmaceuticals, leading sectors of the US economy now operate in a much more densely regulated world than they did before the election of Ronald Reagan, which we usually think of as ushering in an era of deregulation. What did we get in return for this surge in regulation?

II THE ELUSIVE BENEFITS OF THE IP REVOLUTION

Of the various arguments that the advocates of the transformation of IP make, the utilitarian case for restrictions on competition in the production and sale of creative works and inventions is the most superficially powerful one. In an economy where physical capital is decreasingly important, IP advocates argue, intellectual property is the goose that lays the golden eggs of prosperity. That case, however, turns out to be much weaker than its advocates would have you believe.

The case for IP turns on the peculiar economic characteristics of ideas. Because ideas are nonrivalrous (one person's use of an idea does not diminish others' ability to use that same idea) and nonexcludable (once an idea is made public, its originator has no control over who else has access to it), producers of ideas have serious disadvantages (relative to producers of tangible goods) in making money from their intellectual creations. Copyrights and patents remedy this disadvantage by granting temporary monopolies to producers of protected ideas, thus raising the returns to creative expression and innovation.

In other words, copyright and patent laws are regulatory responses to what economists call "market failure." Specifically, if the fixed costs of creative expression or innovation are high, but the costs of imitation are low, artists and inventors would frequently be unable to recoup those fixed costs in the absence of copyright and patents. Accordingly, they would tend to underinvest (from the perspective of total social welfare) in expression and innovation. By allowing producers of ideas to recoup more of the value they create, they "internalize" some of the "externalities" associated with their efforts, thereby better aligning both resource allocation and incentives with maximization of welfare. Or at least that's the idea.

It's a plausible argument with only one problem: the facts on the ground don't provide much support for it. The market failure theory suggests that vulnerability to copying and imitation creates serious disincentives for would-be artists and inventors, such that only exclusive rights over reproduction and use can create the proper incentives for cultural production and technological innovation. Yet we regularly see robust, ebullient creativity and innovation even where intellectual property protections are absent or increasingly porous. The empirical evidence that intellectual property rights stimulate creative expression and innovation is remarkably weak.

Let's look first at creative expression. In the current digital era of nearly costless reproduction and instantaneous global distribution, even increasingly draconian copyright enforcement cannot suppress widespread "theft" and "piracy." Nowhere is the apparent problem more acute than in the recorded music industry, where illegal file-sharing is now rampant. Indeed, since Napster first facilitated mass file-sharing back in 1999, US music industry revenues have fallen precipitously, down 75 percent between 1998 and 2012.[2] Although other factors besides unauthorized copying contributed to this revenue collapse (including the shift in consumer demand from more expensive bundled products, records and CDs, to cheaper singles, and the more recent shift in demand away from buying in favor of streaming), it is generally acknowledged that the rise in illegal copying has depressed sales. Nevertheless, the supply of new music has soared over this period, from 40,000 new albums released in 1999 to almost 80,000 in 2011.[3]

Similar trends hold for both movies and books. In 2014, 707 new feature films were released in the United States, up nearly 40 percent from the 507 films released in 2005.[4] And for books, the number of print titles published by traditional publishers increased 44 percent (from 215,138 to 309,957) between 2002 and 2012, while the number of self-published print book and ebook titles exploded from 85,468 in 2008 to 458,564 in 2013, a more than fivefold increase in just five years.[5]

How can this be? How can a significant decline in effective copyright protection go hand in hand with such a strong surge in creative expression? The same digital revolution that has facilitated unauthorized copying has also slashed the cost of producing creative works. So even if the payoff of hitting the commercial success jackpot has been reduced, the upfront costs of recording an album, making a movie, or publishing a book have fallen as well. Accordingly, the net effect on the financial incentives facing artists may be a wash or even favorable. Furthermore, and more fundamental, the fact is that nonpecuniary considerations predominate in motivating creative expression. The overwhelming majority of creative works don't sell much, but the intrinsic satisfactions of artistic self-expression are so powerful that people will engage in creative pursuits regardless. As society gets richer and more people have the leisure to engage in creative activity, and as new technologies drive down the costs of creative expression, we can expect an ever richer bounty of cultural works no matter what the economic payoffs for a lucky few might be. Strong copyright protection may be important for inflating the monopoly profits of giant media companies, but it is far from clear that it is needed to ensure a vibrant cultural marketplace.

Let's turn now to technological innovation. Here again, empirical evidence doesn't line up well with the market failure theory. To begin with, there is no shortage of innovation in fields where patenting hasn't been an option. Consider, for instance, all the organizational breakthroughs that have helped to power productivity growth since industrialization, including the multidivisional corporation, the R&D department, the department store, the chain store, franchising, statistical process control, just-in-time inventory management, and on and on. All these ideas were quickly and widely imitated, but that was no bar to their original introduction.

Even in areas eligible for patent protection, many firms don't seek patents and flourish all the same. The importance of open-source software to the success of the Internet is a spectacular case in point. Linux now boasts the largest installed base of all general-purpose operating systems, thanks to its use in Android smartphones; Apache servers dominate the World Wide Web; the Perl programming language is used on most websites; the Berkeley Internet Name Daemon (BIND) system is the critical application that connects domain names to numerical Internet Protocol addresses. Meanwhile, a recent study shows that two-thirds of venture capital–backed tech companies have never filed for a single patent. Finally, the electric car manufacturer Tesla, after obtaining patents, decided to give them all away in 2015. Its reasoning was that its patents, by checking competition, were holding back the growth of the electric car industry; by pursuing an open source strategy, it hopes to profit by getting a smaller slice of a much larger pie.

Even if innovation can sometimes thrive in the absence of patents, it may still be the case that patent protection boosts overall levels of innovative activity and thus stimulates technological progress. After all, the extra returns accruing to inventors because of the temporary patent monopoly can be seen as a subsidy for innovative activity, and when you subsidize something you generally get more of it. Despite what would seem like a powerful incentive, economists have struggled to find evidence of patent law's positive effects, in either the United States or elsewhere. Josh Lerner undertook an impressively comprehensive survey, examining 177 different changes in patent policy across 60 countries over a 150-year period. His striking finding was that changes to strengthen patent protection didn't even lead to increased patenting. "This evidence," he concludes, "suggests that these policy changes did not spur innovation."[6] Meanwhile, a study of the 1988 Japanese patent law reform found no evidence that this strengthening of intellectual property protection increased either R&D spending or innovative output. A study of Canadian manufacturing found that firms that use the patent process intensively are no more likely to produce innovations than those that don't. Here in the United States, where patent protections have been broadened and strengthened significantly since the 1980s, one survey of the results led to this muddled conclusion: "Despite the significance of the policy changes and the wide availability of detailed data relating to patenting, robust conclusions regarding the empirical consequences for technological innovation of changes in patent policy are few."[7]

To be fair, the economics literature does offer some support for the benefits of patents. For example, Petra Moser conducted an ingenious historical study by cataloging inventions exhibited at nineteenth-century world fairs and comparing the number of exhibits by and prize medals awarded to various countries (some of which had patent laws at the time, others of which didn't) on a per capita basis. Although she uncovered no evidence that patent laws increased overall levels of innovative activity, she did find that patenting has an influence on the direction of such activity. In countries without patent systems, innovation tended to concentrate in areas where it was relatively easy to maintain secrecy, whereas innovation in patent-law countries was more diverse and broad-ranging.[8] This finding suggests that patents can spur innovation in at least some industries even if the overall effect is unclear.

In that regard, the case for patents is generally thought to be strongest for the pharmaceutical and chemical industries, given their combination of high innovation costs and relative ease of imitation. Indeed, the Orphan Drugs Act of 1983, which offered a number of inducements to develop drugs for rare diseases, including seven years of market exclusivity, provides strong evidence that raising the returns to innovation can accelerate progress. The decade prior to the passage of the act saw the development of only ten new drugs for treating rare diseases; in the decade that followed, the number jumped to 200.[9]

The evidentiary record on patents is thus mixed. Some findings describe positive effects, yes, but there is no convincing confirmation that patent systems as a whole work as intended. Overall, we find ourselves agreeing with the assessment offered nearly 60 years ago by the economist Fritz Machlup, a pioneer in the study of the emerging information economy. "If we did not have a patent system, it would be irresponsible, on the basis of our present knowledge of its economic consequences, to recommend instituting one," Machlup wrote. "But since we have had a patent system for a long time, it would be irresponsible, on the basis of our present knowledge, to recommend abolishing it."[10]

Patent protection's muddled track record shouldn't come as a surprise. The market failure scenario arises only under very specific conditions—namely, high fixed costs of innovation for inventors combined with low costs of effective imitation for their competitors. In such situations, inventors are deterred from investing in innovation because they fear they will not be able to cover their costs. When upfront costs aren't that high and successful imitation isn't that easy, inventors still have adequate incentives to innovate even without temporary monopoly rights. This state of affairs is commonplace, even the norm, as evidenced by robust innovation in domains not eligible for intellectual property protection. Accordingly, it should be expected that patents stimulate innovation only in relatively narrow, exceptional circumstances. The rest of the time, they merely fatten the profits of their holders without creating any extra inducement to innovate.

It's not just that the stimulus to innovation provided by patents is weaker than commonly supposed. In addition, patent protection imposes costs on the innovation process that the market failure theory does not take into account. Most obviously, it raises the prices of patented technologies, which is the whole point of giving patent holders a temporary monopoly. However, higher prices mean reduced demand for those technologies, which in turn means those new technologies diffuse throughout the economy more slowly than they would in a competitive marketplace. The economist Joan Robinson called this the "paradox of patents," which she defined as follows: "The justification of the patent system is that by slowing down the diffusion of technical progress it ensures that there will be more progress to diffuse."[11]

The situation is even more complicated than Robinson describes. It is true that patent protection entails a trade-off between innovation and diffusion, between the inception of good new ideas and their ultimate translation into productivity growth and living standards. There is also another trade-off, which is that patent protection favors "upstream" innovation at the expense of "downstream" innovation. Technological progress doesn't occur in a vacuum; it almost always builds on existing ideas with a series of incremental improvements. When the existing ideas are protected by patents, innovators who seek to build on those ideas may find themselves legally blocked by the requirement to pay steep licensing fees, the inability to obtain the necessary licenses, or infringement actions after the fact if the upstream patents weren't known to the innovators beforehand. Such problems can become especially acute in fields of contemporary technological endeavor, such as biomedicine, semiconductors, and software, where promising innovations may conflict with a whole slew of patents by multiple patent holders. Such "patent thickets"[12] can cause serious coordination and holdup problems that amount to a "tragedy of the anticommons."[13] In the familiar tragedy of the commons, lack of clear ownership rights creates perverse incentives that lead to resource depletion. Here, the mirror-image problem arises, as an excess of overlapping and perhaps conflicting property claims leads to underutilization of resources, especially underinvestment in incremental, sequential innovation.

III THE HIDDEN COSTS OF IP EXPANSION

Notwithstanding the flimsy evidence that intellectual property laws actually fulfill their constitutional mandate "to promote progress in science and the useful arts," those laws have steadily expanded their scope and reach over the years, with explosive growth occurring during the past few decades. The combined effect of those recent expansions has been to throw sand in the wheels of the sectors of the economy with the greatest potential for growth and innovation.

With respect to copyright law, the effects on the Internet are the first place to look for negative impacts on economic growth. Hostility to unauthorized copying in virtually any form, the core principle of copyright law, stands in direct opposition to the logic of the Internet, the greatest technology ever devised for reproducing and disseminating information. Consequently, it casts a pall over the most promising arena for technological and economic progress in the current age. Meanwhile, the runaway explosion in patenting, concentrated in domains where the case for patents is at its weakest, has created daunting obstacles for downstream innovators, especially new entrants who lack the resources to compete in the courtroom as well as in the marketplace.

Copyright law has a long history of antagonism toward technological progress in sharing information more widely and efficiently. Music publishers fought strenuously against first the player piano and then sound recording, arguing that these new methods of bringing music to a wider public were infringing on their rights. (Amusingly, the modern recording industry, now so zealous in defending the sanctity of copyright, was made possible by compromising other copyright holders' claims through compulsory licensing of recording rights.) Broadcasters sued the early cable television industry for appropriating their content and retransmitting it to cable subscribers without paying any copyright royalties; twice they lost at the Supreme Court before Congress stepped in with another compulsory licensing scheme. The film industry sought to kill the videocassette recorder by suing Sony for copyright infringement; the Supreme Court, however, ultimately issued a 5–4 ruling on behalf of Sony. More recently, the recording industry won a Pyrrhic victory against file-sharing of MP3 audio in the celebrated Napster case. Napster was destroyed, but peer-to-peer file-sharing continues unabated.

The principle that all unauthorized copying is legally suspect hangs like the sword of Damocles over the whole Internet, not just file-sharing. When you surf the Web, your computer makes both on-screen and cached copies of the webpages you visit—unauthorized copying. The European Union Court of Justice ultimately ruled in 2014 that this kind of copying does not constitute copyright infringement under EU law.[14] Google makes caches of websites so that they remain accessible to search even if the website is broken or has been taken down—unauthorized copying. A federal district court in Nevada ruled in 2006 that Google's practices are legal.[15] Websites buffer or make temporary copies of small parts of videos so that they will stream smoothly for viewers—unauthorized copying. Every time you forward someone's email, you are engaging in unauthorized copying and are potentially liable (depending on the vague parameters of fair use and implied license) for copyright infringement, with fines ranging up to $150,000 per email. The same kind of potential liability awaits you every time you forward a friend's photos of a party to other friends who attended.[16]

Although we may safely assume that the courts or Congress will prevent copyright law from killing the Internet outright, the current law's antipathy to free information flows ensures that many efforts to realize the Internet's wondrous potential will be hobbled by copyright considerations. Consider the Google Books Library Project, in which the Internet search giant is collaborating with major research libraries to digitize all the world's approximately 130 million books (it has completed about 30 million so far). For books in the public domain, Google Books functions as an online library, with full texts available for reading and downloading. Alas, such books comprise only about 20 percent of the total. For all the rest, including the roughly 70 percent of all books that are out of print but still under copyright, Google Books can offer only brief snippets of text in response to searches, and its right to do that has been vindicated only after a decade of court battles with authors and publishers.[17]

Similar problems afflict efforts to digitize and make publicly available the vast troves of recorded music, film, video, photographs, and artwork currently moldering in library archives. Between automatic copyright protection without formalities and greatly extended copyright terms, vast numbers of "orphan works" now exist whose copyright holders are unknown and unreachable.[18] These works can't be safely reproduced and disseminated because nobody knows whose permission to get first. Although mass digitization holds out the possibility of making virtually everything ever published accessible with a few keystrokes, millions of works continue to languish in limbo simply because of uncertainty over who owns the rights to them.

Meanwhile, access to the vast storehouses of scientific research is bottled up by copyright. A small group of academic publishers, most prominently, Elsevier, Springer, and Wiley, rake in profit margins in excess of 35 percent as subscription prices for university libraries race well ahead of inflation. "Their business model [i]s a marvel," writes copyright historian Peter Baldwin: "Sell scholarship back to the same universities whose scientists had produced, written, peer reviewed, and edited it largely for free."[19] An enterprising neuroscience researcher in Kazakhstan created the website Sci-Hub to breach the academic publishing paywalls for some 47 million journal articles. Predictably, the website was shut down by a US federal court in October 2015; just as predictably, the website popped up soon afterward under another name, and is also accessible on the "dark web."[20] Thus does copyright law, established to promote science, push scientific research into the same digital underground utilized by purveyors of weapons and child pornography.

Even as copyright law undercuts the Internet's promise, it simultaneously heightens the risks associated with the digital revolution. In particular, the anti-circumvention provisions of the Digital Millennium Copyright Law raise serious legal obstacles for outside security researchers who probe for vulnerabilities to viruses and theft. As a result, resources and expertise available to help keep our data and devices safe are sidelined by the quixotic effort to quash file-sharing, with potentially dire consequences.[21]

With regard to patent law, the idea that more patent protection should lead to more innovation has been put to the test and found severely wanting. If patents truly incentivize innovation in the way that supporters claim, the shift to stronger and more expansive patent protection should have been accompanied by an upsurge in technological breakthroughs. So what has been the payoff from a fivefold increase in patenting over 30 years? The most comprehensive measure of innovation, total factor productivity growth, offers no evidence of a patenting dividend. After a temporary spike from 1996 to 2004, TFP growth has sunk back to the low rates typical during the 1970s and 1980s even as the number of new patents issued every year has continued to soar.

Indeed, more fine-grained analysis offers good reason to believe that the patenting explosion has been harmful for many innovators. Research by James Bessen and Michael Meurer compared the estimated value of public companies' patent portfolios to the estimated cost of defending patent cases during the 1980s and 1990s. In particular, they divided the public companies they studied into two groups: chemical and pharmaceutical firms, on the one hand, and all other firms, on the other. For both groups, the cost of defending patent cases began rising sharply in the mid-1990s. For chemical and pharmaceutical firms, the value of their patent holdings remained clearly greater than those litigation costs, approximately $12 billion in value compared with roughly $4 billion in costs as of 1999. For all other industries, however, the situation was reversed. By 1999, litigation costs had soared to around $12 billion, whereas the total value of their patent holdings was only $3 billion. In other words, outside the chemical and pharmaceutical industries, American public companies would apparently be better off if the patent system didn't exist.[22]

A major part of the problem lies in the differences between chemical and pharmaceutical patents and most other kinds of patents. For the former group, the scope of patents is clearly and precisely delineated by chemical formulas. Accordingly, it is relatively straightforward for subsequent innovators to discover whether their new products are covered by any existing patents. By contrast, the scope of other kinds of patents, especially new-style patents for software or business methods, is described by abstract language that is invariably open to differing interpretations. This vagueness in the boundaries of intellectual property, combined with the immense number of patents in force at any one time, make it virtually impossible for downstream innovators to be sure whether the new products they are developing are infringing on someone else's patents. One study estimates that it would take two million patent attorneys working full time just to check every software-producing firm's new products against all the new software patents issued in a given year; alas, there are only 40,000 practicing patent attorneys in the country.[23] As a result, the patent system can act as a vast and uncharted minefield through which innovators must pass at their peril.

The dysfunctions of the patent system have been exacerbated in recent years by the rise of so-called patent assertion entities, better known as "patent trolls." Patent trolls are firms that neither manufacture nor sell products but instead specialize in amassing patent portfolios for the purpose of initiating infringement lawsuits. According to a White House report, lawsuits by patent trolls tripled between 2010 and 2012 alone, as the share of total patent infringement suits initiated by such firms rose from 29 percent to 62 percent.[24] That's right: most patent infringement suits are now brought by firms that make no products at all and whose chief activity is to prevent other companies from making products. A 2012 study found that the direct costs of defending patent troll suits (i.e., lawyers' and licensing fees) came to $29 billion in 2011. To put that figure in context, it amounts to more than 10 percent of total annual R&D expenditures by US businesses.[25]

The threat of such predatory behavior has given rise to the practice of "defensive patenting," seeking patents for one's own products or amassing portfolios of others' patents in the hope of protecting oneself from infringement suits. Suitably well-armed, corporate giants can use the threat of mutually assured litigation to negotiate cross-licensing deals. At that point the companies are in the same position as if none of them had any patents, with one important exception: members of the cross-licensing club can wield their patent portfolios to fend off competition from new entrants who dare to challenge their oligopoly.

IV THE IP INEQUALITY MACHINE

The current state of intellectual property law may be bad for economic growth overall, but it is highly effective at showering riches on a favored few. In the entertainment, software, and pharmaceutical industries, the monopoly power created by copyright and patent protections encourages industry concentration, inflates corporate profits, and exaggerates the tendency toward winner-take-all "superstar markets."[26] As a result, income and wealth are even more highly concentrated at the top than would otherwise be the case.

There is a natural winner-take-all dynamic in the entertainment industry. The vast majority of books, records, and films generate very small sales while a lucky few become huge hits. To take an extreme example, Adele's latest album, 25, accounted for an astonishing 42 percent of total music sales during the week of its release.[27] If there were no copyright law, the artist and original distributor of one of these lucky jackpot winners would receive income from sales, but so too would other distributors that moved in once it was clear that the work was in high demand. Because of copyright, all sales are captured by a single distributor, and the price per unit sold is substantially higher as well because of the lack of competition. Since copyright law gives distributors monopolies over popular works, the income generated by those works is much more highly concentrated than it otherwise would be.

The copyright monopoly, combined with ever-lengthening copyright terms, affects the whole structure of the entertainment industry. The financial stakes in discovering and effectively marketing the next runaway bestseller with enduring appeal are enormous. Success means the creation of a cash cow that can sustain corporate profits for many decades. It is unsurprising, then, that the industry has come to be dominated by a few media giants: four record labels (Sony BMI Music, Warner Music Group, EMI Music Group, Universal Music Group) account for roughly 85 percent of US recorded music sales and 70 percent of the global market, while five movie studios (Walt Disney, Paramount, Sony, Twentieth Century Fox, Universal Pictures, and Warner Brothers) have captured around 80 percent of the US market and 75 percent globally. As copyright terms have lengthened (and, simultaneously, global markets have grown by leaps and bounds), the industry has become progressively organized around the maximization of returns from the occasional runaway crowd favorite. This task requires large-scale investments in talent search and marketing for success in the long term, which means developing a diversified portfolio of new talent and a growing inventory of cash cows to milk as efficiently and as long as possible.

Neither software nor pharmaceuticals can match the entertainment industry for its extremes. On one end, there is an enormous volume of low-selling books, records, and films; at the other end, many blockbusters remain bestsellers for decades. But like entertainment, these other information-intensive industries are shaped by powerful economies of scale. In all these industries, the upfront fixed costs of producing the first copy of a product are high while the variable costs of producing additional copies are low. The larger the sales volume, the more sales there are over which fixed costs can be spread and for which the unit costs of production will be lower. For pharmaceuticals, these scale economies are amplified by the high upfront costs of securing FDA approval; for software, they are ramped up by network effects (software used by many people can be much more valuable than software used by only a few). These factors push in the direction of high levels of inter-firm inequality within these industries; in other words, high levels of concentration in which a few firms account for the vast bulk of sales and profits.

Pushing in the other direction, however, is the vulnerability of companies in these industries to relatively easy imitation. Open competition would allow new entrants that did not have to incur all the heavy fixed costs of the first mover and that could therefore sell profitably at a much lower price. These new entrants would drive down prices and take market share away from the first mover (although significant first-mover advantages still remain).

Strong intellectual property protection—copyright for entertainment, patents for drugs, and a combination for software—eliminates or at least reduces this threat of copycat competition. Accordingly, the effect of patents and copyright is to allow industry leaders to take fuller advantage of the potential scale economies that the nature of their industries permits. The result is even higher levels of inter-firm inequality than would otherwise be possible, with industries dominated by a few highly profitable giants.

The computer/software industry has featured a succession of such giants, with Microsoft, Apple, Google, and Facebook topping the list. Concentration in the pharmaceutical sector has been checked to some extent by the rise of generic drug producers and biotech startups, but still a merger wave in recent decades has produced the huge companies now known as "Big Pharma." As a result, the market share of the top ten firms in the industry jumped from around 20 percent of global sales in 1985 to 48 percent by 2002.[28] The profitability of the sector is abnormally high, with average operating margins around 25 percent, compared to 15 percent or less for other consumer goods producers.[29]

The enormous aggregations of market capitalization and profits in the IP-intensive industries then translate into soaring wealth and incomes for shareholders, employees, and professionals. Most obvious are the vast fortunes made in entertainment and the Internet sector, but the effect on economic inequality is considerably broader than the mind-boggling payouts for those at the very top of the income scale. Because these industries are skill-intensive (i.e., their employees are more highly skilled than the workforce as a whole), any pass-through of rents to workers in the form of higher wages will go mainly to more highly educated and highly paid employees. The effect then is to further increase the growing inequality between the highly skilled and everybody else.

V THE FLAWED MORAL CASE FOR IP

Why has the protection of intellectual property expanded so promiscuously given its very large negative consequences for economic growth and the distribution of income and wealth? Like many other policies, intellectual property protection is not justified simply on utilitarian grounds, any more than freedom of religion or speech are. The expansion of intellectual property protection has been justified because, like these other rights, its advocates could make a moral claim on its behalf. This remains a very influential argument, especially among conservatives. If it were persuasive, it would be a reason to ignore, in whole or in part, the distributive and economic growth effects of IP protection, just as we typically don't scrutinize the distributive effects of freedom of religion.

But despite its wide acceptance, the claim that copyright and patent holders are merely receiving their rightful due rests on reasoning that's shaky at best. Indeed, the moral principle that supposedly grounds that claim is regularly violated by the laws in question.

The expression "intellectual property" came into general usage only during the past few decades—during the same period, perhaps not coincidentally, that copyright and patent protections have expanded so dramatically.[30] The term is accurate enough in a technical sense because copyrights and patents are tradable entitlements to exclusive rights over particular forms of wealth, namely, expressive works and inventions, and thus can fairly be considered forms of property. Then again, equally accurate would be the term "intellectual monopoly," as copyright and patent laws create legal monopolies to engage in particular economic activities (i.e., making certain uses of protected expressions or inventions).[31] Needless to say, the choice between the two terms is not rhetorically neutral. Monopoly has a clearly negative connotation, whereas property suggests, well, propriety. The rise of the expression "intellectual property" has aided the waxing fortunes of its referents by moralizing what they do in favorable terms: the laws in question exist to give their beneficiaries not special privileges, but merely their rightful due.

In the United States, the moral case for the recognition and enforcement of intellectual property, the claim that copyright and patent holders deserve the special legal protections they receive, grows out of John Locke's famous labor theory of appropriation.[32] According to Locke, private property originates in people's ownership of their own bodies and thus their own labor. People deserve to enjoy the fruits of their labor, so when they mix their labor with material objects by possessing them or working to improve them, they establish valid claims to use, control, and consume those things. They become owners, and the things become their property.

The Locke-inspired theory of intellectual property extends this reasoning from the world of tangible stuff to the incorporeal world of ideas. People own their own minds, and thus they deserve to enjoy the fruits of their mental labor. So when they write a new book or a new song, or they devise a better mousetrap, they mix their mental labor with material objects and thereby become owners of their creations.

This theory starts on solid enough footing. People certainly ought to be able to make use of their own ideas, or not, as they see fit. Authors should be able to sell books they write to publishers, and inventors should be able to build and sell their new contraptions. Who else could possibly have a better claim to do so? Likewise, they should be able to keep their ideas secret or share them with other people of their own choosing on the condition that those recipients keep the secret. To this extent, at least, it makes perfect sense to talk of artists and inventors as the owners of the ideas they originate.

To justify copyright and patents, however, the Lockean theory must be extended further. In this more expansive view, ownership of ideas extends to controlling the use of ideas after they have been made public. When people buy a copyrighted book or patented invention, they own only the hardware of that purchase, the specific tangible object. The software, the arrangement of the words in a book, the design or production process that made the invention possible, remains the property of the copyright or patent holder. Nobody else can make use of that software without the owner's permission.

The moral case for copyright and patents thus proceeds on the assumption that there are two different levels of entitlement to the fruits of one's mental labor. Employing the familiar metaphor of ownership as a bundle of rights, we can call these two levels the basic bundle and the premium bundle. The basic bundle authorizes people to make use of and decide whether and how to disseminate the ideas they originate. Basic ownership is universal, meaning it applies even when the ideas in question are not eligible for copyright or patent protection. In addition, there is an expanded form of ownership that applies in certain delimited circumstances. This premium bundle of rights, institutionalized in copyright and patent law, gives property holders exclusive rights over the ideas they originate even after they have been disseminated. In other words, it authorizes property holders to prevent others from making use of those ideas or to control how they do so.

There are serious conceptual difficulties with fleshing out this two-level approach to ownership of ideas—specifically, distinguishing between those products of mental labor that qualify for premium protection and those that don't. There are large domains of intellectual effort that are not eligible for copyright or patents under current law, including scientific discoveries, fashion, jokes, new artistic themes or styles, new forms of business, and so on. It is challenging, to say the least, to discern any coherent principle that determines which intellectual products receive basic or premium protection and explains why those that receive the latter are so deserving.

In our opinion, the biggest problem with the moral case for patents and copyright laws is that those laws as currently constituted regularly violate the principle on which they are supposedly grounded—namely, entitlement to the fruits of one's mental labor. The exclusive rights granted to copyright and patent holders aren't just an additional premium layer of protection on top of the basic rights that all enjoy. Rather, copyright and patent laws extend premium rights to some in a way that frequently restricts the basic rights of others. Perversely, copyright and patent laws are regularly used to stop people from producing or selling their own original works.

This was not always the case with copyright. Originally, US law prohibited only simple copying of full works as originally published. Thus, translations and even abridgments were not considered infringing. Gradually, the concept of infringement expanded to cover so-called derivative works—for example, a play based on a book, or a book that contains characters created by another author. This expansion was checked, to a limited and uncertain extent, by the concurrent rise of the doctrine of "fair use." According to this doctrine, some derivative works—parodies, for example, and books that include brief quoted passages from other works—are not considered infringing. For everything else, including adaptations of an artistic work to a new format, new works using existing literary characters or settings, remixes or mashups of musical works, and so forth, the restrictions and penalties of copyright apply. In all these cases, artists can expend mental effort to create something new and original, but they are not allowed to publish or sell it.[33] They are thus deprived of their basic rights to the fruits of their own mental labor.

In the case of patent law, independent invention has never been a defense against claims of infringement. As a result, inventors who come in second in a patent race have no right at all to make use of and profit from their ideas. This is by no means an unusual occurrence, for nearly simultaneous and completely independent discovery of new technologies occurs with astonishing frequency.[34] Indeed, patent infringement lawsuits only rarely involve intentional copying of someone else's invention; in the clear majority of lawsuits, the alleged infringers developed their products on their own and weren't even aware of the patent in question.[35]

In summary, the moral case for patents and copyright is supposedly based on the entitlement to enjoy the fruits of one's mental labor. Yet under current law, the most basic and universal form that this entitlement can take, one whose general propriety is completely uncontroversial, is regularly traduced. We therefore find unconvincing the claim that copyright and patent holders are rightful property owners who are only receiving their just due. Yes, we can imagine intellectual property laws in which the moral claims for exclusive rights are much stronger. If copyright were limited to its original concern of preventing sales of full reproductions, and if patents were awarded to all independent co-inventors (or at least independent invention were a complete defense in any infringement action), then intellectual property rights would indeed provide additional protections for artists and inventors without impinging on the basic rights of other artists and inventors. But that is not the intellectual property law we have today, and to get there would require major statutory changes.

The copyright and patent laws we have today therefore look more like intellectual monopoly than intellectual property. They do not simply give people their rightful due; on the contrary, they regularly deprive people of their rightful due. If there is a case to be made for the special privileges granted under these laws, it must be based on utilitarian grounds. As we have already seen, that case is surprisingly weak, and utterly incapable of justifying the radical expansion in IP protection that has occurred in recent years. Therefore, it is entirely appropriate to strip IP protection of its sheep's clothing and to see it for the wolf it is, a major source of economic stagnation and a tool for unjust enrichment.

OCCUPATIONAL LICENSING

IN OUR FIRST TWO CASE studies we examined high-profile areas of federal policy that oversee major industries composed of gigantic global enterprises. Many of the companies and leaders in these sectors are household names. All the relevant policy decisions are made in Washington, DC, and the stakes are enormous: the implications of a single critical policy choice can run from billions of dollars to threatening the economic well-being of the whole world. The prominence of the issues, the centralization of the decision making, and the magnitude of the issues combine to ensure that policy disputes are hot topics of national debate, subject to incessant journalistic coverage and in-depth academic study.

Now it is time to leave the spotlight for the shadows. Our next two case studies, occupational licensing and land use, look at relatively obscure areas of state and local policy. None of the relevant actors are famous at the national level. Decisions are made in fifty state capitals and thousands of local jurisdictions. The resolution of any particular policy dispute is usually of concern only to the specific parties involved while the impact on the larger economy is obscure. For these reasons, the policy areas in question have been all but invisible in the national policy debate.

In recent years, a small but growing body of academic research has revealed that this inattention, however understandable, has been costly. It turns out that the decentralized, small-scale policy processes of occupational licensing and land-use regulation sum up to weighty national significance. Both impose barriers to entry: mandatory licensing, in the economist's sense of impeding entry by new firms or individuals into a product market; zoning restrictions, in the literal sense of hindering physical entry into a geographical area. Spreading and growing steeper in recent decades, these barriers to entry now constitute significant constraints on innovation and growth. Licensing blocks competition from the new firms that are frequently the vessels of more productive ways of doing things; zoning, by attenuating urban density, weakens an important catalyst for the creation of new ideas while frustrating efforts to bring those ideas to scale. Meanwhile, licensing and zoning are significant contributors to the rise in economic inequality. While these policies do not result in the truly massive, narrow concentrations of corporate or individual wealth that we saw in finance and intellectual property, the thumb they place on the scale for the "merely affluent" is just as important.

I THE GROWTH OF THE LICENSED ECONOMY

The decline of private-sector unionism since the 1970s has been one of the biggest economic stories of this era, and its causes and effects have been extensively studied and hotly debated. Scarcely noticed, meanwhile, was the rise of a very different form of labor market regulation over the same period: occupational licensing, or the requirement to obtain a government license before being legally permitted to do a particular job. Such requirements are usually imposed at the state level, although there is some federal and local licensing as well. While union membership and density faltered and ultimately collapsed, occupational licensing took off. The percentage of private-sector workers in a union dropped from 29 percent in 1970 to under 7 percent today, even as the percentage of workers subject to a licensing requirement jumped from 10 percent to almost 30 percent.[1]

The rise of licensing is due in part to the changing composition of the workforce—specifically, the increasing share of workers employed in the heavily licensed fields of education, healthcare, and law. But about two-thirds of the increase in licensing's coverage reflects the spread of licensing requirements to more and more occupations.[2] Comprehensive data are sketchy, but it is estimated that more than 1,100 different jobs are now subject to licensing requirements in at least one state.[3] Everybody is familiar with the state licensing of doctors and lawyers, but other commonly regulated occupations (subject to licensing in at least 30 of the 50 states and the District of Columbia) include cosmetologists (licensed in 51 jurisdictions), manicurists (50), barbers (50), preschool teachers (49), athletic trainers (46), massage therapists (39), makeup artists (36), and auctioneers (33). Other regulated occupations include animal breeders (licensed in 26 jurisdictions), taxidermists (26), gaming dealers (24), animal trainers (20), sign-language interpreters (16), bartenders (13), landscape contractors (13), funeral attendants (9), upholsterers (7), interior designers (4), and florists (1).[4]

Occupational licensing is typically justified on the grounds of consumer protection. By setting minimum qualifications to ply a particular trade, the government can weed out the incompetent and unethical to ensure that consumers aren't ripped off or physically harmed. However, basic economic theory makes clear that, at best, licensing helps some consumers at the expense of others. Assuming (and, as is shown a bit later, this assumption has little empirical basis) the criteria used to screen applicants are well designed to distinguish between competent, reputable service providers and bad apples, the effect of licensing will be

to raise the overall quality of supply. It does not follow, however, that licensing will thereby also raise overall consumer welfare. After all, restricting supply can be expected to raise prices,
which means that some consumers will no longer be able to
afford the service in question. Accordingly, the best that occupational licensing can accomplish is to benefit some consumers at the expense of others. Some more quality-conscious (and
presumably higher-income) consumers are better off, but some
more price-conscious (and presumably lower-income) consumers are worse off.[5] Even if it works as well as it can, occupational
licensing is thus regressive in its distributional consequences.

Meanwhile, licensing regimes and the requirements they
impose are all too often highly arbitrary. If the existence of occupational licensing were really a response to underlying market
failures (e.g., information asymmetries) that made consumers
especially vulnerable to abuse, the same types of occupations
would be regulated in state after state. In reality, the scope of
occupational licensing is all over the place. Although more than
1,100 different occupations are licensed at the state level, the
highest number of occupations licensed in any one state is 177
(California takes this dubious prize).[6] This fact strongly suggests that factors other than industry characteristics determine
who gets regulated.

Similarly, if licensing requirements were really highly relevant to supplier quality, you would expect to see similar requirements across states for any widely licensed occupation. In fact,
the stringency of regulation varies wildly within industries. Take
manicuring, for example, licensed in 49 states and the District
of Columbia. The average number of days of required education
and training nationwide is 87, but actual requirements range
from 163 days of education and training in Alabama to only
9 days in Iowa and 3 days in Alaska.[7] Here again, considerations
besides consumer protection seem to be driving the level of
regulation.

Furthermore, the variation in regulatory stringency across industries looks arbitrary as well. You might expect that the strictest forms of regulation are reserved for industries in which potential consumer harms are the worst. How then to explain the fact that cosmetologists must complete an average of 372 days of education and training before getting their license while emergency medical technicians, who frequently deal with matters of life and death, must complete on average only 33 days?[8]

It should come as no surprise that empirical studies discover little or no connection between occupational licensing and better service for consumers. A study of dentistry by University of Minnesota economist Morris Kleiner found no evidence that patients in states with stricter regulation experienced improved outcomes—whether as measured by dental exams of new Air Force recruits, complaints filed with state licensing boards, or malpractice insurance rates.[9] Other research by Kleiner has failed to establish any link between licensing and better outcomes for either mortgage brokerage or child-care services.[10] An examination of schoolteachers found that imposition of state testing requirements did not improve the quality of teachers as measured by their educational backgrounds.[11] Researchers studying Louisiana's licensing of florists conducted an interesting experiment: 25 floral arrangements from Louisiana and 25 arrangements from neighboring and unregulated Texas, all randomly selected, were examined by a randomly selected panel of 8 florists from Texas and 10 from Louisiana. The judges gave virtually identical scores to the Texas and Louisiana arrangements; moreover, the licensed Louisiana florists and unlicensed Texas florists differed little in their ratings.[12] Another study found that Florida's relaxation of licensing restrictions on roofers following Hurricanes Frances and Katrina did not reduce the quality of roofing services despite the fact that asymmetric information problems, frequently cited to justify licensing, could be expected to be especially severe in a post-crisis environment.[13]

II THE PRICE OF INCUMBENT PROTECTION

Occupational licensing may not offer much in the way of consumer protection, but it succeeds admirably as protectionism, shielding incumbent firms from competition and thereby boosting their incomes at consumers' expense. It works much better than the classic form of protectionism, tariffs, which restrict foreign supply but leave domestic supply untouched. Accordingly, although the imposition of a new trade barrier will temporarily boost domestic industry profits, those profits will lead new firms to enter the market or existing firms to boost capacity, and eventually profit margins will subside. Occupational licensing, by contrast, restricts all supply, and as a consequence the benefits it confers persist over time.

So how effective is occupational protectionism? Bear in mind that the rigor of licensing requirements, and thus the "height" of the barrier, varies widely both by occupation and state. According to Kleiner and Princeton economist Alan Krueger, occupational licensing is associated with 18 percent higher wages on average.[14] This boost in pay is the result of restricting supply. For occupations licensed in some states but not others, employment growth is 20 percent lower in the restrictive states.[15] Consumers, instead of being protected, are stuck with the bill because prices for licensed services are inflated anywhere from 5 percent to 33 percent, with the cost to consumers amounting to some $203 billion a year.[16]

This cost isn't just a zero-sum transfer from consumers to license holders. By inflating the price of regulated services, licensing leads to underconsumption of those services and a shift in spending to less highly valued products. Economists call the drop in output caused by such a misallocation of resources a "deadweight loss," and in the case of occupational licensing a 2006 estimate pegged this loss of output at around $40 billion.[17]

The sacrifice in output due to deadweight loss is just the tip of the iceberg when it comes to the economic costs imposed by occupational licensing. The main damage inflicted by licensing is its ongoing interference with entrepreneurship and innovation, the engines of economic dynamism. While misallocating resources causes a one-time reduction in the level of output, undermining dynamism can result in a permanently slower rate of economic growth.

In Chapter 2, we discussed how entry barriers throw sand in the gears of "creative destruction." That ceaseless churn of firm entry and exit is a central element of the innovation process, given that new firms are so frequently the means by which new products and new ideas are introduced to the world. Research shows that surviving new firms are generally more productive than existing firms, while existing firms have higher productivity than those that go out of business. Occupational licensing, by impeding the formation of new businesses, slows down this vital channel of productivity growth.

The advent of app-based ridesharing firms like Uber and Lyft, and the furious resistance they often provoke from supporters of the traditional taxicab industry, offer a powerfully vivid illustration of the conflict between occupational licensing and innovation. The quality of taxi services has long been fodder for consumer grumbling, but improvement through competition was thwarted by restrictive taxi licensing and associated anticompetitive regulations. When ridesharing firms devised an ingeniously convenient new way to purchase rides for hire, and an ingenious end-run around the current regulatory structure, consumers leaped to take advantage. One report found that by 2015, Uber accounted for 46 percent of paid car rides by business travelers in major markets.[18] The market has declared unambiguously that regulation is not necessary to ensure safe, convenient rides. In fact, a recent study puts the consumer surplus (the difference between what riders would have been willing to pay and what they actually paid) generated by UberX in 2015 at $6.8 billion.[19] Meanwhile, existing taxi companies are now rushing to mimic their new competitors, offering their own apps and expanding the availability and convenience of payment by credit card. A study of New York and Chicago shows that rate of consumer complaints against taxi drivers have fallen since Uber came on the scene.[20]

The harm caused by occupational licensing goes beyond higher prices, misallocated resources, and lost growth. In addition, licensing widens the gap between rich and poor by squelching employment opportunities for people at the lower end of the socioeconomic scale and by inflating the compensation of highly skilled professionals at the top of that scale.

As mentioned above, licensing has a negative effect on employment. Indeed, that's the whole point, to erect legal obstacles of mandatory fees and training in order to reduce the supply of providers in the licensed field. The toll in lost jobs is substantial; nationwide, total employment is down by as many as 2.85 million jobs because of licensing.[21] Much of the growth in licensing during recent decades has occurred in less-skilled occupations. Accordingly, even as employment prospects for the less skilled have dwindled generally because of automation and globalization, the spread of licensing has further aggravated the situation.

For one thing, licensing narrows the job choices open to people who didn't graduate from college: 43 percent of people in licensed occupations are required to have a college degree, but only 32 percent of Americans have one.[22] Licensing requirements can be especially daunting for members of ethnic minorities. For example, a study of teacher testing found that it did nothing to improve the quality of teachers as measured by their educational background, but it did lead to fewer Hispanic teachers.[23] And a study of the licensing of manicurists found that English proficiency requirements reduced the number of Vietnamese manicurists per capita, as well as the number of manicurists overall.[24]

Licensing further blocks opportunities for the disadvantaged by disqualifying applicants who have any sort of criminal record. It is common for licensing laws to treat any past arrest or conviction as an absolute bar to obtaining employment, even when the prior offense has no bearing on qualifications for the occupation in question. Beth Avery of the National Employment Law Project found, for example, that in Alabama "a land surveyor is stripped of his license if convicted of any felony, anywhere in the country, even if completely unrelated to the profession."[25] Given that roughly one third of all Americans have a police record of some kind, this punitiveness puts many job opportunities completely out of reach for a large fraction of the workforce.[26] Because of the much higher rate of criminal justice involvement of African Americans, the licensing-incarceration connection swells the nation's large racial income gap, while also increasing recidivism by blocking the option of legitimate careers after criminals have done their time.

As we will discuss in further detail in the following chapter, upward social mobility often hinges on geographic mobility. Since economic opportunities aren't evenly distributed across the country, pursuing opportunities sometimes requires moving to a new location. Yet, the patchwork of state-based occupational licensing requirements erects significant barriers against moving out of state, since a license in one state is frequently not valid in the rest of the country. To assess the impact of licensing on geographic mobility, Kleiner and Janna Johnson compared interstate and intrastate migration rates for workers in five widely licensed occupations. They found that licensed workers, while they moved in-state at roughly the same rate as similar workers in other occupations, were much less likely to move out of state.[27] Here then is yet another way in which occupational licensing makes it harder for Americans struggling to get ahead.

Even as licensing stifles opportunities for the less advantaged, it fattens rewards for those at the top. Although licensing inflates compensation for low-skill and high-skill occupations alike, the effects are most pronounced in the high-income, high-status professions—think doctors, dentists, optometrists, and lawyers. As Kleiner notes, this means that the effect of licensing overall is to increase income inequality. "Since occupational licensing appears to increase earnings, on average, for persons in high income occupations relative to persons in low income ones," Kleiner writes, "this state and local policy may serve to exacerbate income dispersion in the United States."[28]

At this point, we want to leave behind this panoramic analysis of licensing as a whole. Since our focus in this book is on policies that undermine growth while providing rents for the rich, we will home in now on the licensing of elite professions, including doctors and dentists in healthcare and attorneys in legal services. In all these professions, mandatory licensing is one element of a larger system of rent extraction, one that encompasses not only restricting the supply of practitioners but also inflating demand for their services. The end result is higher prices, worse service, stunted innovation, and large and ill-gotten gains for groups that crowd the upper percentiles of the income scale.

III THE HIGH COST
OF MEDICAL LICENSING

What to do about spiraling healthcare expenditures has been a central topic in the national policy debate for decades. Furthermore, it is common knowledge among experts that America's record-setting level of spending, now exceeding 17 percent of GDP, reflects not only higher utilization of services than elsewhere but also significantly higher prices for those services. In particular, it is widely known that doctors in the United States earn much more than their counterparts in other countries. Given that doctors are the second-largest occupational category in the top 1 percent of income, their outsized pay is a big part of the story of American inequality.[29]

Despite all this, the role of licensing has been largely ignored in the debate on spiraling healthcare costs. The apparent explanation is that nobody can imagine that there is any alternative. The complexity of modern medicine, the need for extensive training to master that complexity, and the harms that can be inflicted by incompetent physicians all lead to the seemingly obvious conclusion that state screening of physicians is inescapably necessary. In fact, even critics of the expansion of licensing into areas like cosmetology are usually careful to point out that doctors should, obviously, be licensed. This point of view was encapsulated in an exchange between Justices Stephen Breyer and Antonin Scalia in a recent Supreme Court case that addressed the composition of state licensing boards for dentists. During oral argument Breyer observed, "I would like brain surgeons to decide [who can perform brain surgery in this state]." Scalia, no stranger to dissent, found nothing to disagree with. "I want a neurologist to decide," he added.[30]

A strong status quo bias is understandable here; after all, state licensing of doctors has been around for more than a century. When looking at the situation with fresh eyes, it is striking how little in the way of genuine consumer protection the current licensing system provides. Indeed, there are good arguments that existing policies actually reduce the overall quality of American healthcare.

Let's start with the fact that Justices Breyer and Scalia were incorrect in thinking that state licensing decides who can perform brain surgery. A medical license entitles its holder to practice medicine generally; no specialties are licensed by the state. Complete an approved residency program in the United States in podiatry, pass the state medical examination, and you are legally authorized to do brain surgery, heart transplants, or any other procedure you wish. Given how specialized medicine is these days, a state medical license is therefore not a reliable indicator of relevant competence in a wide range of critical, life-or-death situations.

Furthermore, medical licensing's stringent requirements are imposed only on those entering the profession. Since a career can span many decades, during which time best practices frequently change in dramatic fashion, the mere possession of a license offers little assurance that large numbers of practicing doctors are actually competent. Yes, licensing boards do have the power to suspend or revoke licenses as well as issue fines and reprimands, but the actual discipline imposed by such boards is notoriously lax. Of doctors who made at least 10 separate malpractice payments between 1990 and 2005, only one third received any kind of discipline from their state medical boards. When sanctions are imposed, they are usually for illegally prescribing drugs, substance abuse, or inappropriate behavior with patients, not simple incompetence.[31]

Virtually all the real quality screening that does occur is performed by the private sector. Private specialty boards certify competence in particular practice areas. Practice groups and health maintenance organizations decide which physicians to hire, while hospitals decide which physicians will be granted admitting and surgical privileges. These decisions about employment and affiliations are made with a view toward burnishing and safeguarding reputation and minimizing exposure to liability.

In particular, the looming threat of malpractice liability, and the consequent need to acquire insurance, creates strong incentives for greater quality. Insurance premiums are heavily experience-rated, meaning they go up sharply for physicians who have to pay claims. Malpractice insurers offer discounts for participation in risk management programs; they impose surcharges for things like failed board examinations and failure to obtain hospital privileges. They can even restrict a physician's practice or require supervision or more training. Despite claims from conservatives and the medical profession that the system is out of control, there is good evidence that malpractice awards are in line with actual damages and little evidence that a so-called liability crisis is driving doctors out of practice or forcing them into wasteful defensive medicine.[32] All told, normal commercial motives for providing good service, backstopped by the courts and malpractice insurers, do much more to protect the public from bad doctors than anything accomplished by state medical boards.

There is a strong case to be made that state licensing actually reduces the overall quality of healthcare. A fascinating study of Soviet physicians who immigrated to Israel, some of whom were required to take an exam to get a medical license while others were exempted, showed that the exam requirement actually resulted in "negative selection," or a reduction in physician quality.[33] In the face of an onerous entry barrier, the strongest performers with the most attractive career options are more likely to be deterred from entering the profession.

In addition, licensing can reduce the quality of healthcare provision by constricting the supply of doctors, raising their fees, and thereby inducing people not to go to the doctor. Instead, they rely on self-help or seek out some non-mainstream but more affordable alternative. By reducing the number of qualified physicians and thereby boosting the market share of homeopaths, nutritional supplement hawkers, crystal therapists, and other assorted quacks, licensing pushes the overall quality of healthcare downward.

While failing to serve the interests of patients well, medical licensing is very effective in boosting physicians' incomes. A 2008 study compared the salaries of American doctors to those of their counterparts in Australia, Canada, France, Germany, and the United Kingdom. Pre-tax earnings for U.S. primary care physicians averaged $186,600 (in 2008 dollars), 54 percent higher than the average of $121,200 for the other five countries. At the top of the pay scale, American orthopedic surgeons averaged $442,500, more than double the $215,500 average for the benchmark countries.[34] Doctors overall are extremely well represented among the top 1 percent of earners, with 21.5 percent having membership in the club.[35]

Most analysis of American doctors' lavish pay focuses on the demand side—in particular, heavy reliance on third-party payment (whether by private insurers or the government through Medicare and Medicaid) that renders the actual consumers of healthcare (patients) indifferent to costs at the point of sale, as well as the continued dominance of a "fee for service" payment model that effectively rewards doctors for inefficiency. But supply-side factors play an important role as well. First of all, the rigorous training and examination requirements imposed by state licensing act directly to impede entry into the medical profession. Furthermore, these entry barriers are buttressed by limits on who can provide the necessary training.

Under state licensing laws, the American Medical Association is vested with the authority to provide accreditation for U.S. medical schools, and accreditation is limited to a particular class size. Thus the medical profession controls how many newly minted MDs are produced in the country every year. From 1980 until around 2005, the number of medical school slots was frozen at around 16,000 first-year students; since then, expansion has brought the number above 20,000.[36] Although graduation from a U.S. medical school is not required to obtain a medical license, completion of a U.S. residency program is (in contrast to other advanced countries, which regularly license foreign-born physicians who did their training abroad). The U.S. residency requirement, combined with highly restrictive policies on high-skill immigration, makes AMA power over medical school accreditation a powerful lever to constrict supply. Meanwhile, by historical accident the vast bulk of funding for residency slots is provided by Medicare, and for cost saving reasons the number of slots has been frozen since 1997. In 2016, for example, 8,640 graduates of accredited medical schools who applied for residencies—or roughly a quarter of all applicants— failed to be given a match.[37] The consequence is that, at a time when there is a desperate need for more general practitioners, thousands of graduates of medical schools are prevented from becoming doctors.[38]

The final layer of supply control consists of laws against the unauthorized practice of medicine. Here physicians have lost some ground in recent decades as midlevel healthcare professionals—physician assistants, nurse practitioners, and midwives—have won the right to perform many functions previously reserved for M.D.s. The liberalization remains patchy; currently, just 21 states and the District of Columbia allow nurse practitioners to diagnose and treat patients and prescribe medication without a physician's supervision. Meanwhile, efforts are underway to boost education requirements for midlevel professionals, so entry into these fields may be more restricted in the future. Despite its limits, an expanded role for midlevel professionals can make a real difference. According to a study by

Morris Kleiner and others, restrictions on the ability of nurse practioners to prescribe medicine translate into an increase in doctors' earnings of up to 7 percent.[39]

The regulation of entry into the dental profession follows the same general pattern as that for doctors. All dentists must graduate from an accredited dental school in the United States, with the limited exception that some schools in Canada have also been approved. A commission operating under the auspices of the American Dental Association performs accreditation. Dentists must also pass a licensing exam, whose relative rigor has much more to do with improving earnings for dentists than improving outcomes for patients. A study by Morris Kleiner and Robert Kudrle examined differences in pass rates among the states to gauge the effect of entry regulation. They estimated that dentists in the most restrictive states earned 12 percent more than their colleagues in the least restrictive states; however, they were unable to find any evidence that the quality of care was higher in the more restrictive states.

Like American doctors, American dentists make much more than their counterparts do around the world. According to a recent survey, dentists in the United States earn 40 percent more on average than those in Japan, the next highest paid country, and over twice as much as dentists in the United Kingdom and Finland. As of 2014, the average pay for dentists in the United States was $201,900, while the median was $170,000.[40] That's enough to put 15 percent of dentists in the top 1 percent of earners.[41] Since third-party payments for dental care are much less extensive than for medical care, supply restrictions through licensing probably play a relatively greater role in explaining the pay premiums of dentists than they do for doctors.

Like doctors, dentists police restrictions on supply through scope-of-practice regulations that reserve certain tasks for licensed members of their profession. As with the case for doctors, the boundaries of those tasks that only dentists can perform have been the subject of ongoing skirmishes with other licensed professionals—in particular, dental hygienists. Hygienists have gradually been winning greater autonomy, and that has cut into dentists' rents. According to a study by Morris Kleiner and Kyoung Won Park, granting hygienists the right to be self-employed reduces dentists' earnings by 16 percent.[42]

IV LAW, LICENSING, AND LUCRE

No other occupational group, nor any interest group for that matter, can rival the legal profession in its rent-seeking capacity. Other groups can utilize superior organization, favorable policy image, venue selection, and other strategies to capture the policymaking process on those narrow slivers of issues that directly concern them. American lawyers, by contrast, have put themselves in a position to exert excessive and undue influence over the policymaking process *in toto*. Lawyers are wildly overrepresented in the ranks of legislators. Only 0.6 percent of the adult population, they constituted 41 percent of the 113th Congress. They are likewise disproportionately prominent among executive branch officials in charge of enforcement, and of course virtually all judges are lawyers. Thus, at every step of the process—making the law, carrying it out, and interpreting what it means—lawyers have influence far out of line with their numbers.

It is therefore wholly unsurprising that the current state of public policy is very kind to the interests of the legal profession. Like many other occupational groups, lawyers have used licensing to limit supply. In addition, they use their strong presence in policymaking, policy execution, and policy interpretation to inflate demand for their services by creating a legal and regulatory system whose byzantine complexity serves no one's interest but their own.

Like doctors and dentists, lawyers impose two layers of screening to control entry into their profession. First, in every state but Wisconsin it is necessary to pass a rigorous bar examination in order to receive a license to practice law. The protectionist function of this requirement was revealed by a telling study that looked at variations in pass rates for state bar exams. Researchers found that pass rates are highly correlated with potential supply; in other words, states with more people trying to pass the bar tend to have tougher exams.[43] Meanwhile, in all but a few states, it is necessary to graduate from a law school accredited by the American Bar Association before being allowed to sit for the bar exam.

The legal profession then defends the integrity of this double wall of entry barriers with strict regulations on the unauthorized practice of law. For example, LegalZoom has faced legal challenges from eight different state bar associations as it has sought to build its business of providing inexpensive legal assistance online.[44] In addition, ABA regulations impose other restrictions on who can provide legal services. In particular, lawyers who work for firms not owned and managed by other lawyers cannot provide legal services for anyone outside their firm. Accordingly, only traditional law firms may provide legal services to the public, as opposed to, say, business service companies that provided legal assistance along with other professional services.

In addition to maintaining these elaborate mechanisms for limiting supply, the legal profession extracts rents by inflating demand for its services. There is no self-conscious strategy at work here; rather, the disproportionate influence exerted by lawyers over the policymaking process leads naturally to policies shaped by adversarial proceedings and characterized by abstruse and bewildering technical detail.[45] From the mind-numbing complexities of the tax code to the lax rules for allowing class-action lawsuits, the result is heavy dependence on high-priced legal expertise to navigate the artificial and gratuitous complexities of the legal environment.

Thus do we arrive at this seemingly paradoxical state of affairs. While the United States has far more lawyers per capita than other countries, American lawyers nonetheless earn a sizable premium relatively to members of equivalently skilled occupations. The United States boasts a much higher number of lawyers per capita than almost all other countries in the world; as of 2006 there were 3.05 lawyers per thousand capita in the United States, compared to 2.50 in the United Kingdom, 2.21 in Canada, 1.68 in Germany, and 0.72 in France.[46] Nevertheless, according to a careful study by Brookings Institution scholars, American lawyers earn a sizable premium that cannot be attributed to skills or personal characteristics. In other words, their high pay includes sizable rents. That earnings premium stood at around 25 percent back in the late 1970s and has risen to roughly 50 percent more recently. This premium reflects the combined effects of supply-constricting and demand-inflating government policies.[47]

While the average American may think of Warren Buffett and Mark Zuckerberg when they envision the top 1 percent, it is actually the surgeon who replaced their hip, the dentist who performed their last root canal, or the lawyer who handled their divorce who are the more typical representatives of that elite demographic. What they all have in common is that their incomes are substantially inflated by occupational licensing. At the same time, licensing has well-hidden negative impacts on the economically less advantaged, increasing the prices they pay for services, closing them out entirely from whole sectors of the economy, and increasing the costs they pay to move up economically. The face of inequality, in short, is as likely to be a highly protected professional as the plucky entrepreneur that apologists for surging inequality typically point to.

LAND USE

HOME OWNERSHIP HOLDS A SPECIAL place in the American cultural imagination: it offers independence, a refuge from the world, and an opportunity to amass capital. A complex web of policies, from the mortgage interest deduction to the creation of the 30-year, fixed-rate mortgage, have been enacted with the justification of making this part of the American dream real. In practice, these policies have had the effect of redistributing upward, enriching higher-income homeowners and the bankers who provide mortgage finance.

Here we will examine another set of policies that redistribute wealth and income to homeowners: zoning and other forms of land-use regulation. Although zoning has been around for a century, its effects remained local and small-scale until recently. In the past few decades, however, land-use regulation has become a major constraint on new housing supply, especially in the most dynamic, high-growth cities in the United States.

For most of American history, when growth and opportunity in a particular place led to greater demand to move there, the supply of housing responded. Cities became denser, creating space for newcomers to share in the opportunity provided by the places graced by fortune. The returns to landowners were constrained by the entrance of new housing supply on the market.

In the last few decades, this process has ground to a halt. Incumbents in the most expensive housing markets in the country, such as San Francisco, Los Angeles, New York, and Boston, have become increasingly successful at stopping the creation of new housing. By preventing supply from responding to rising demand, they have artificially boosted housing prices in those markets, creating a windfall for existing homeowners. In the process, they have also made it harder for newcomers to move into cities with surging incomes, pushing them to parts of the country with less opportunity.

The beneficiaries of this form of upward redistribution are much more numerous than the notorious 1 percent who benefit from subsidies for financial leverage or intellectual property protection. Like occupational licensing, constraints on land use redistribute to the merely affluent, not just the extraordinarily wealthy. And the aggregate costs of this relatively widespread kind of regressive rent-seeking are staggering. The inability of millions of Americans to move to where opportunity is puts a huge brake on economic growth, and constrains the historic engine of economic mobility provided by geographic mobility.

I THE STRANGLED URBAN HOUSING MARKET

Comprehensive controls on land use through zoning and other restrictions emerged in the United States early in the twentieth century and became endemic as the century progressed. The theoretical justification for zoning is that it coordinates orderly economic development and sanitary living conditions by geographically segregating conflicting and possibly incompatible land uses. What the common law of nuisance dealt with after the fact, zoning would prevent through prudent regulation.

In practice, the rise of zoning had little to do with the prevention of physical nuisances. Rather, the driving impetus was the protection of property values in neighborhoods of single-family homes from the threat of nearby nonconforming uses, whether in the form of industrial or commercial facilities or high-density apartments (and their poorer and darker residents). The suburbanization of America led to the zoning of America, with land-use controls operating as a kind of surrogate for home value insurance.[1]

From the beginning, zoning exerted a powerful influence on the location and character of housing supply within a given metropolitan area. That was the whole point. Up until around 1970, however, zoning does not appear to have affected the growth of aggregate housing supply across such areas. Housing may have been artificially restricted in some affluent suburbs, but more concentrated growth in development-friendly communities kept overall housing supply in the larger region responsive to growth in demand.

Harvard economist Edward Glaeser, together with colleagues, has led the way in amassing evidence of how things have changed since 1970. The first clue is the growing gap between house prices and construction costs. Between 1950 and 1970, house prices grew in line with construction costs; real house prices per square foot rose 35 percent over the period while inflation-adjusted construction costs per square foot increased by 28 percent. Between 1970 and 2000, by contrast, house prices shot up by 72 percent while construction costs actually declined by 3 percent. The divergence has been especially dramatic in America's big coastal cities. While real construction costs in Boston and San Francisco rose by 6.6 percent and 5.6 percent, respectively, house prices shot up by 127 percent in Boston and 270 percent in San Francisco.[2]

Can improvements in the quality of new homes explain the gap? To investigate, Glaeser compared trends in home prices overall to trends in repeat sales (which hold home quality constant) and found that changes in quality can explain at most a quarter of the increase in house prices nationwide. In high-price cities, quality improvements have been even less of a factor.[3]

The next clue is that house prices rose relative to costs even as the rate of new construction has declined. Looking at a sample of 102 metropolitan areas, Glaeser found that the median rate of new construction (new homes divided by initial housing stock) fell from a robust 40 percent during the 1950s to only 14 percent during the 2000s. This decline has been especially dramatic in high-price coastal cities. In the 1950s, the housing stock grew by more than 20 percent in New York, over 30 percent in San Francisco, and almost 60 percent in Los Angeles; in the 2000s, on the other hand, the rate of new construction in all three metropolitan areas fell well below 10 percent.[4]

The conventional explanation for skyrocketing home prices on the coasts is that land for new housing construction is scarce. These cities have many amenities that make them desirable places to live, the thinking goes, but they are already heavily built up so there is not much potential for further expansion of the housing supply. If the conventional wisdom were true, one would expect to find that metropolitan areas with the highest home prices also have the highest densities (residents per square mile). As Glaeser found, very little relationship exists between house prices and density. For example, densities are comparatively low in many parts of Boston despite very high house prices, and although prices have climbed rapidly in recent decades, density hasn't increased much.[5]

One additional clue comes from comparing the prices of land, depending on whether it sits under a house or simply extends the lot of another house. The former can be estimated by backing construction costs out of house prices to infer the price of the land; the latter can be estimated by comparing the sale prices of similar homes located on different-sized lots. Interestingly, the former calculation yields land values about 10 times greater than those generated by the latter calculation.[6]

This striking disparity suggests that the price of a house actually consists of three elements: construction costs, the value of the land, and the added element of the value of the right to build on that land.

It is the escalating value of that third element, which Glaeser calls the "regulatory tax," that has driven up housing prices in many of America's big urban areas. The rate of the regulatory tax has been climbing because of the progressive tightening of land-use restrictions. According to Glaeser's calculations, the regulatory tax caused by land-use controls varies widely across the country. In a review of 21 different urban areas, Glaeser found that the regulatory tax is minimal in 10 of them. In Baltimore, Boston, and Washington, DC, it climbs to roughly 20 percent. In Los Angeles and Oakland, it surpasses 30 percent. In Manhattan, San Francisco, and San Jose, the regulatory tax has reached roughly 50 percent.[7]

Zoning has always been about the extraction of rents, in both the everyday sense of that word as well as the specialized way the word is used by economists. The overriding purpose of land-use regulation has been to protect homeowners' property values at the expense of access to housing for everybody else. In other words, zoning exists to transfer wealth from new buyers to existing owners. In recent decades, the scale of those transfers has grown markedly, especially in the country's big coastal cities.

II ZONING OUT ECONOMIC GROWTH

How exactly is this rent extraction bad for growth at the national level? Even if zoning restrictions are growing progressively worse in big urban areas, the United States remains a largely empty country. If people are priced out of building or living in one location, alternatives always exist. Yes, zoning alters where people choose to live, but how does the location of America's population affect prospects for expanded output and higher incomes?

It turns out that most of our country is empty for a very good reason: people derive great value from concentrating together in urban areas. First, proximity reduces transportation costs, so producers benefit from being close to their suppliers and customers. Second, more people living in one place means deeper and more diverse markets for both products and labor. With a large enough urban population, niche markets that appeal to only a small fraction of consumers become profitable to serve. Employers have a better pool of potential workers to draw from, while workers have greater choice in prospective employers. Third, people living and working close to one another can take advantage of "information spillovers" in which cities expand opportunities for exchanging ideas and information, thereby facilitating both innovation and the accumulation of human capital.

Economists call these benefits of urban concentration, which combine economies of scale and network effects, "economies of agglomeration." For most of history, these centralizing forces were held in check by the requirements of traditional, low-productivity agriculture. Growing food required not only lots of open land but also relatively large numbers of people to work that land. As the mechanization of agriculture freed people from work on the farm, the gravitational attraction of cities asserted itself. In 1900, when 40 percent of Americans still worked on farms, just under 40 percent of the population was located in urban areas. By 2010, with fewer than 2 percent of the workforce employed in agriculture, a full 81 percent of the population now lived in cities.

All cities are not created equal. Whether due to natural factors (e.g., climate, proximity to bodies of water) or accidents of history (e.g., William Shockley moved to northern California to take care of his ailing mother and thereby set in motion a train of events that would result in Silicon Valley), some urban areas end up with much higher populations, output, and output per worker than others. Thus, as of 2005 the top 50 most productive metropolitan areas in the United States (out of a total of 363) combined to produce 60 percent of the nation's GDP. Meanwhile, in the top ten cities the unweighted average of output per worker exceeded $91,000, more than double the average of just under $40,000 in the country's ten least productive metro areas.[8]

These big differences in productivity translate into big differences in incomes. We normally think of income inequality as a function of differences in class or socioeconomic status, such that workers in high-skill occupations with high levels of educational attainment make more than workers with less education and lower skill levels. Much more than generally realized, geographic differences are also a major source of inequality. Indeed, geographic inequality can sometimes outweigh the more familiar socioeconomic inequality. For example, the average income of high school graduates in Boston is now over 40 percent higher than the average income of college grads in Flint, Michigan.[9]

Geographic inequality tends to be self-liquidating when people can move from poorer areas to richer areas. Wage differences across cities and regions, by creating incentives for moving, spur an arbitrage process whereby those wage differences are reduced and overall output and wages rise. The people who relocate make a lot more than they did before, boosting overall output and wages. By reducing labor supply in lower-income areas (thereby putting upward pressure on wages there) and boosting labor supply in higher-income areas (thus putting downward pressure on wages), they also work to smooth out income differences rooted in location. Under these circumstances, geographic mobility produces social mobility, and the same moves that reduce inequality simultaneously increase economic output.

Through much of the twentieth century, geographic mobility was a significant contributor to both income convergence and economic growth. Between 1880 and 1980, per capita incomes in US states converged at an average rate of 2 percent a year.[10] In other words, per capita incomes in poorer states rose faster than in richer ones. Many factors worked together to produce this result, but one was labor mobility; over this period, people moved on net from poorer to richer areas. These dynamics had strongly egalitarian consequences; in fact, approximately one-third of the decline in hourly wage inequality between 1940 and 1980 was due to cross-state convergence.[11]

Mobility was also an engine of growth. The lure of higher wages in the innovative, high-productivity cities of the Northeast and industrial heartland led to explosive population gains in those cities. Between 1870 and 1950, New York City's population grew over 700 percent, Chicago's climbed over 1,100 percent, and Detroit's population skyrocketed by over 2,200 percent. In analyzing the productivity gains from industrialization, economists regularly stress the important role played by reallocating labor from low-productivity agriculture to high-productivity factory and office jobs. Much of this move from one economic sector to another was accomplished by a physical move from one place to another. The sectoral and spatial reallocation of labor from less productive to more productive uses went hand in hand.

In recent decades, this reallocation process has sputtered and broken down. According to Harvard economists Peter Ganong and Daniel Shoag, between 1990 and 2010 the rate at which income gaps across states narrowed was less than half the long-term historical rate.[12] With the shift from an industrial to an information economy, the innovative, high-productivity cities of today are no longer manufacturing hubs. Rather, the cities that now feature big wage premiums, and which therefore should attract big influxes of new workers, are human capital hubs, urban areas with large numbers of college graduates. Unfortunately, these very same cities have led the way in constraining housing growth with ever more restrictive land-use regulation.

Since the 1970s, college graduates have increasingly tended to congregate in particular urban areas—namely, those that started out with initially high shares of college grads. In other words, education levels in American cities have diverged over time. The smart cities get smarter while other cities fall farther and farther behind. To illustrate this phenomenon, Enrico Moretti of the University of California, Berkeley, cites the examples of Albuquerque, New Mexico, and Seattle, Washington. As it just so happens, the former metro area is where Microsoft was founded in 1975, while the latter has been the company's headquarters since 1979 (when Bill Gates and Paul Allen made the fateful decision to move back to their hometown). Back in 1970, the cities looked similar in terms of human capital levels. The number of college grads relative to population was only 5 percent higher in Seattle than in Albuquerque. By 1990, though, the gap had grown to 14 percent, by 2000, it had swollen to 35 percent, and as of 2012, it stood at 45 percent.[13]

The contrast between the most educated and least educated cities in the United States is now truly remarkable. In the five top human capital hubs, the average share of workers with a college degree or better was 49 percent as of 2006–08; among the bottom five metro areas in the rankings, the average rate of college completion among workers was only 12 percent. To put the disparity in perspective, this four-to-one ratio is equal to the difference between the college completion rates in the United States overall and Ghana.[14]

The increasing geographic concentration of highly skilled workers is a response to those economies of agglomeration we discussed earlier—in particular, the information spillovers that accelerate skill acquisition and innovation when smart people work together in close proximity. Because of agglomeration economies, metro areas with higher population densities generally have higher productivity levels and incomes.[15] It turns out, though, that the degree to which density raises productivity varies with human capital levels. Specifically, in cities with a human capital stock one standard deviation above the mean, the productivity-boosting impact of extra density doubles relative to the mean; however, for cities with a human capital stock one standard deviation below the mean, the productivity boost from density disappears altogether.[16] In other words, when a city manages to attract a lot of high-skill workers, more people and more density means especially big payoffs in increased productivity.

Those payoffs don't just benefit college grads. Less-skilled workers in the city are even bigger winners, in part because they provide services to lots of affluent managers and professionals who can afford to pay them high wages. Let's look again at the top five and bottom five metro areas in terms of share of college-educated workers. In the top five, college grads earn an average annual salary of $87,689 as of 2006–08, 61 percent more than the average salary of $54,518 earned by college grads in the bottom five. By comparison, high school grads in the top five make $71,483 a year on average, a whopping 137 percent more than their counterparts in the bottom five.[17] According to calculations by Enrico Moretti, a percentage point increase in a city's share of college-educated workers boosts the earning of college grads in that city by 0.4 percent and lifts the earnings of high school grads by 1.6 percent, or four times as much.[18]

America's innovative, high-productivity human capital hubs should be experiencing rapid population growth as both highly skilled and less-skilled workers flock there in search of higher pay and wider opportunities. But they are not. In recent decades, migration flows in the United States have gone in the opposite direction, away from the richer coastal cities and toward the poorer exurbs of the Sunbelt. To take an especially striking example, consider the more recent experience of San Jose, California, the heart of Silicon Valley. Between 1995 and 2000, at the height of the dizzying Internet boom, 100,000 more native-born Americans moved out of the San Jose metro area than moved in.

In his 2011 book *The Gated City*, Ryan Avent of *The Economist* refers to this inversion of traditional migration patterns as "moving to stagnation." Avent documented this phenomenon by comparing two groups of American cities, which he labeled as "gainers" and "losers." For the gainers, he identified the 10 metropolitan areas with population above 1 million that enjoyed the largest domestic in-migration between 2000 and 2009: Phoenix, Riverside, Atlanta, Dallas, Las Vegas, Tampa, Charlotte, Houston, Austin, and Orlando. For the losers, he selected the five metropolitan areas with populations above 1 million that boasted the highest average wages in 2000: New York, San Francisco, San Jose, Boston, and Washington, DC. These two groups are roughly comparable in size. In 2009, the combined population of the gainers came to 36.5 million while that of the losers totaled 35.3 million. Between 2000 and 2009, the losers lost almost as many out-migrants on net as the gainers welcomed in-migrants, with 3.3 million net in-migrants to the gainers and 2.9 million net out-migrants from the losers.

These strikingly unusual patterns of population movement represent a flight from opportunity. In 2009, the average wage in the losers was $64,228, compared with only $47,539 in the gainers. Even as Americans were moving away from them, the loser cities were increasing their wage advantage. Average wages grew by $13,786 in those five cities between 2000 and 2009, compared with only $10,973 in the 10 gainer cities.[19]

Why move away from higher and faster-growing wages? The answer is clear: housing costs. The rise of the Sunbelt has been a major demographic story of the post–World War II era, but the plot of the story has taken a big twist in recent decades. As Edward Glaeser has documented, between 1950 and 1980, population gains in the Sunbelt were propelled primarily by above-average productivity growth. Since 1980, however, the rapid growth in the Sunbelt's housing supply, and thus its growing advantage in offering affordable housing, is the main factor behind the region's continuing attractiveness.[20]

Meanwhile, in the high-productivity human capital hubs that should be growing robustly, artificially high housing costs act as a regressive filter. Since housing costs bulk larger in the budgets of less-skilled, lower-income workers than for the highly skilled and well paid, those costs have a differential impact in deterring in-migration. Even though the gross wage premium for college grads is smaller than it is for high school grads, the situation changes when you look at wages net of housing costs. High-income workers still enjoy a net wage premium and thus still have an incentive to move, but for less-skilled workers, the regulatory tax on housing wipes out any wage premium. As a result, college grads continue to move to human capital hubs, while less-educated workers, who would stand to gain the most by moving, are kept away by artificial housing scarcity.[21]

Enrico Moretti, working with Chiang-Tai Hsieh of the University of Chicago, has produced the best estimate thus far of the cumulative impact these local distortions have on the national economy. Their analysis reveals that the scale of these distortions, and the combined toll they haven taken, are staggeringly large. When you look at wages across metropolitan areas (as opposed to across states or regions), there has been no convergence at all over the past half century. On the contrary, there has been sizable divergence because geographic inequality has gotten dramatically worse. Specifically, Moretti and Hsieh find that the standard deviation of wages across US cities in 2009 was twice as large as it was in 1964. This worsening spatial misallocation of labor has exacted a stiff price. The increasing dispersion of wages has reduced total US economic output by an average of 0.3 percentage points a year. In other words, if the dispersion of wages as of 2009 were the same as it was in 1964, the US economy would be 13.5 percent larger than it is at present.

As to the cause of growing geographic inequality, Moretti and Hsieh conclude that the main culprit is land-use restrictions. Truly striking is that the lion's share of the harm is being caused by the highly restrictive policies of just three cities: New York, San Francisco, and San Jose. If regulatory barriers to new housing construction in those three cities had been pared back to just the median level of restrictions nationwide, Moretti and Hsieh estimate that the resulting influx of workers would have raised overall US output by 9.7 percent over the period in question.[22]

With land-use regulation, slumping growth and rising inequality are inextricably connected. It is precisely through perpetuating and entrenching geographic inequality that potential economic output is squandered. The inegalitarian consequences of zoning go beyond exacerbating income differences across cities. The regressive nature of zoning begins with its animating purpose, to protect homeowners' property values by making it more difficult and expensive to build additional housing in the area. Putting aside the ultimate effect on mobility across cities, the direct effect of zoning within any given city is to transfer wealth from renters to homeowners. Since homeowners generally have both higher incomes and higher net worth than renters, this amounts to upward redistribution from the less affluent to the more affluent.[23]

Zoning's exclusionary means add insult to the injury of its regressive end; zoning accomplishes its objectives by keeping poor people away from rich people. That insult, in turn, results in further injury to disadvantaged communities. Evidence points unsurprisingly to a connection between zoning and residential segregation along both ethnic and socioeconomic lines.[24] Such segregation is a major factor in perpetuating disadvantage from one generation to the next.[25]

By discouraging moving, zoning is one of a number of factors (the expansion of occupational licensing is another) behind the pronounced drop-off in residential mobility in recent decades. Since the 1980s, the percentage of people who have moved in the past year, whether to another county or another state, has fallen sharply.[26] Mobility rates vary by educational level. High school grads, for instance, are less likely to move than college grads, and high school dropouts are the least likely to move. This gradient along educational and socioeconomic lines is nothing new, but what is new is the rising cost of staying put. According to Scott Winship, the income gap between people who have moved across state lines at least once in their lives and those who haven't has widened substantially since the 1970s. Moreover, the divergence in fortunes between movers and non-movers has been particularly pronounced among people who grew up in low-income households.[27]

Zoning's suppression of mobility isn't just bad economic policy. It's also bad social policy, deepening economic disadvantage by deterring people from seeking out better opportunities elsewhere. Especially perverse is how the restrictiveness of zoning has been on the rise even as the social costs of immobility have been climbing as well.

Finally, zoning's contributions to economic inequality go beyond widening income gaps, whether geographic or socio-economic in nature. In addition, tightening restrictions on building appear to be the driving force behind rising wealth inequality. At least that is the conclusion of Matt Rognlie, who as a 26-year-old grad student at MIT leaped to prominence with his bold critique of Thomas Piketty's bestselling *Capital in the Twenty-First Century*. Piketty famously argued that there is a fundamental tendency in capitalism toward ever-greater concentration of wealth, a tendency that was checked in the twentieth century only because of global depression and war, and then only temporarily. Specifically, he argued that over the long run, the rate of return on wealth tends to outstrip the rate of economic growth, with the result that the share of national income that compensates owners of capital grows inexorably (and the share that goes to workers shrinks concomitantly).

In the United States (as well as elsewhere), recent decades have indeed seen a rise in capital's share of national income. When Rognlie broke down the aggregate figure of capital income into its component elements, he found that only one component was responsible for the overall rise: housing wealth.[28] While the dark sorcery of hedge fund managers and other plutocrats plays a role in the spike in income inequality, it is runaway home prices that have fueled the rising returns to capital.

III THE BIG PICTURE OF REGRESSIVE REGULATION

So what conclusions can we draw from these four case studies? One clear observation is that regressive rent-seeking is a real and growing problem. Even if the phenomenon is limited to the four policy areas discussed here (and it most certainly is not!), it is creating major distortions in some of the most important sectors of the American economy: finance, mass media and entertainment, healthcare, legal services, and housing. In all four areas, the trajectory of policy change in recent decades has been toward ever-greater rent extraction. In finance, subsidies for excessive risk-taking have expanded dramatically with the advent and metastasis of "too big to fail." In intellectual property law, the scope of monopoly privileges has grown by leaps and bounds. As to occupational licensing, the percentage of total employment caught in its web has nearly tripled. With regard to zoning, restrictions on the construction of new housing, especially in the big coastal cities, have become draconian in their rigor.

The pileup of rents represents the perverse triumph of political entrepreneurship. Narrow interests have profited by deftly exploiting opportunities inherent in the country's current stage of economic development. In all advanced economies, services constitute an ever-growing component of both output and employment as productivity growth in the other sectors (agriculture and manufacturing) races ahead of demand. Growing demand for services means more money for service providers, but an increasing number of providers have diverted even more money their way by blocking entry into their occupations with licensing requirements. Along similar lines, mass affluence has ensured a rising share of healthcare spending in national income. As the necessities of food, shelter, and clothing grow ever cheaper, and the array of life-extending technologies continues to expand, people naturally shift their spending toward prolonging their lives and improving their physical well-being. Drug makers (through patent protection) and healthcare professionals (through occupational licensing) have exaggerated their gains from this rising demand by using the political process to constrict supply.

In the rapidly growing information technology sector, the presence of strong network effects in information technology guarantees that some industries will feature "winner take all" markets with high levels of concentration. Lobbyists for strong copyright and patent protection for software have further amplified this dynamic by fortifying the winners' market power with additional barriers to entry. Meanwhile, network effects have also led to geographic concentration, as highly skilled knowledge workers are increasingly congregating together in "human capital hubs." As a result, a few big coastal cities have come to account for an outsized share of the nation's productive capacity, as well as its opportunities for upward mobility. Homeowners in those cities would have profited handsomely in any event, but they have multiplied their winnings by pulling up the drawbridge with increasingly restrictive land-use regulations,

The opportunistic parasitism of regressive rent-seeking has hit the twenty-first-century American economy at its most vulnerable points—namely, its twin susceptibilities to slowing growth and rising inequality. Even if rent-seeking could be eliminated altogether, deep-seated and powerful forces would still cause the economic pie to grow more slowly and its sustenance to be shared less evenly. The aging of the population and the exhaustion of possibilities for rapid improvement in educational attainment and women's labor force participation already meant that growth would slow in the absence of a surge in productivity growth. With the rise of policies that suppress and distort competition in key sectors, productivity growth has been hampered instead of encouraged; consequently, the country's growth outlook is now even cloudier. At the same time, increasing inequality was powered by a number of different factors, including the rise of IT, women's increasing labor market opportunities, and the return of mass immigration. A large-scale political project to siphon off further resources and funnel them to the rich was the opposite of what was needed, yet that is what we got.

In short, our case studies show the rise of policies that deliver the maximum benefit for a favored few while inflicting maximum harm on everybody else. Which raises the question, How could this happen? What is it about our political system that made it so vulnerable to capture by narrow interests? What is it about the particular narrow interests in question that made them so successful in playing the political game to their advantage? For some answers, let's move on to the next chapter.

THE POLITICS OF

REGRESSIVE STAGNATION

THE STORY TOLD IN THE previous chapters is a depressing one. Regressive rents are deeply embedded in our economic system. They reduce the dynamism of our economy at the very time when productivity is already slumping, slowing firm formation and making it harder for new innovations to disrupt existing business models. At the same time, upward redistribution exacerbates America's accelerating income inequality, which is the last thing we need when so many other trends in American society are pushing in the same direction.

While upward redistribution is one of the central political problems of our time, it is no accident. It is the result of numerous, overlapping political forces that, in combination, make it easier to create and defend regressive rents than to stop or reverse them. Many of the causes of regressive rent-seeking are generic features of our political system that apply to all concentrated interests but which are particularly toxic when organization is combined with wealth.

Democracy is inherently vulnerable to rent-seeking. That does not mean, as many conservatives and libertarians have argued, that the only way to limit abuses is to drastically shrink the size and scope of government. That position is a nonstarter, as the vast majority of Americans consider such a cure to be much worse than the disease. Furthermore, it obscures the fact that there is huge variation across countries, levels of government, and policy areas in the degree to which special interests dominate the policy process. Since some policymakers are much more successful than others in resisting capture by the interests they regulate, it follows that the causes of failure are more specific than the existence of democracy and activist government, and that remedies for those specific maladies can be fashioned. Some rent-seeking may be inevitable in a modern democratic welfare state, it is true, but the current high level of rent-seeking is not.

While democratic government is inherently vulnerable to predation by narrow, well-organized interests, the specific structure of the policymaking process can help to reduce this vulnerability, or it can make it even worse. In particular, democracy is best able to protect itself from exploitation by the powerful when it is most deliberative in character. Officials in democratic systems can resist the claims by the powerful for special favors but only when those claims are brought out into the open and subjected to serious scrutiny.

What characterizes all the areas of rent-seeking described in the previous chapters is that, in one way or another, democratic deliberation has broken down. The problem of narrow interests' advantages in organizing and wielding influence is always with us, but it is especially severe in the cases at hand where the interests are so flush with resources. Furthermore, we identify four additional sources of bias that stack the deck even more in favor of the rent-seekers. The first source of bias is information asymmetries, in which the government's dependence on regulated interests for policy-relevant information makes it especially open to capture. The second involves the exploitation by rent-seekers of a favorable "policy image" that short-circuits appropriate scrutiny of their self-serving claims. The third source of bias concerns the venue of decision making: when policies are crafted in obscure or insular settings that discourage monitoring and participation by outsiders, it becomes all the more likely that policymaking will be captured by insiders. Finally, the fourth source of bias is the pronounced tendency of American public policy toward "kludgeocracy—" indirect approaches to addressing social problems that funnel resources through the private sector and allow rent-seekers to skim off some of the flow.

In this chapter, we lay out the various ways in which deliberative breakdown can open the way for rent-seeking. In Chapter 8, we point to some of the ways to rebuild democracy's deliberative capacity and reduce its vulnerability to exploitation by the powerful.

I THE TYRANNY OF THE ORGANIZED

Over a half-century ago, the economist Mancur Olson identified rent-seeking as an inherent defect in democracy.[1] Olson argued that concentrated interests—those for whom a change in government action would make a large impact on their material well-being—would be relatively likely to organize. By contrast, diffuse interests (including those that pay the costs of programs for concentrated interests) would be difficult if not impossible to organize. As the old lottery ad said, "You can't win if you don't play." The organized "play" by showing up when decisions are made, providing valuable information to policymakers, engaging in surveillance of government, and letting policymakers know that they will notice if their interests are not served.

Concentrated interests do not always defeat diffuse interests, but when this game is repeated thousands upon thousands of times, you end up with a government that is mainly in the business of serving the already organized. Once groups do actually obtain some benefit from the state, the ability to organize them goes up considerably, since it is easier to organize people to keep what they already have than to get something they haven't enjoyed yet.[2] Once the group has extracted resources from the state, it can recycle some of them into further political activity and into the pockets of organizational leaders who have a strong material interest in seeking out new benefits that will justify their existence. Carried on long enough, such dynamics lead to what Jonathan Rauch calls "demosclerosis."[3] The multiplication of mobilized rent-seeking groups gums up the economy, slowing the process of eliminating existing, inefficient firms to make room for new, more efficient ones.

Concentrated benefits and diffuse costs go a long way toward explaining many of the outcomes described in the preceding chapters. Occupational licensing provides an obvious case in point. For, say, cosmetologists, discouraging competition by piling up onerous training requirements can deliver a sizable boost to earnings; by contrast, the dispersed consumers who have to pay a few more dollars at the salon don't have a big enough stake in the issue to organize and fight back. While a potential organizational entrepreneur might try to organize them, it would be an uphill battle just to identify these consumers and get them to contribute to collective action.

Likewise, consider zoning. Homeowners in a given community share a strong interest in preserving their property values (typically the largest asset they own), their proximity to one another makes it relatively easy to form bonds and socially sanction those who may disagree with them, and they reside, pay taxes, and vote in the jurisdictions whose land-use regulations they want to influence. By contrast, the people who pay the cost of constrained housing supply include all the potential house buyers in a metro area who face higher prices or are priced out, but who often are not even citizens of the jurisdictions that are making the rules.

A similar story can be told about intellectual property. The holders of intellectual property, such as drug companies protecting patents and entertainment firms attempting to extend copyrights, have the viability of their whole business model riding on the state of the law. Those hurt by overly aggressive IP protection, such as patients paying more for drugs, may not even know that their prices are being impacted by legal rules. Even if they did, the price they pay is so low per transaction that no organizational entrepreneur is likely to think it worth organizing them to pay the costs of fighting these rules.

With stakes like this on the table—the earning potential of a line of work, the value of a house, the profits and executive compensation of a huge industry—rent-seekers rarely fail to recognize their common interest, and they are willing to invest in politics up to the value of the benefit they are protecting. Those stakes, as the previous chapters have shown, are in the billions of dollars, which means that even a small segment of wealthy rent-seekers can justify participating in politics.

Olson did not frame his analysis of the problem in terms of democratic deliberation, but his analysis can be used to illuminate our problem of deliberative breakdown. Our constitution was designed not simply to reflect popular impulses but also to "refine and enlarge" them through the operation of institutions. The Constitution does that in part by separating institutions and making it difficult for a majority faction to work its will. This, the framers thought, would force statesmen to actually have to persuade one another, as well as truck and barter.[4]

However, real deliberation, which we loosely define as due consideration of public policy on something like the merits, is not as genteel a process as the word may seem to modern ears. Deliberation—whether it occurs in Congress, federal governmental agencies, state legislatures, or city councils—requires organized, effective citizen activity to force legislators to open up the agenda to new forms of information and alternative framing of problems.

In most of the cases in this book, rent-seeking thrives as a consequence of issues being entirely off the agenda, or characterized by one-sided participation. As Baumgartner, Berry, Hojnacki, Kimball, and Leech argue, imbalanced policy outcomes are typically generated by policy domains in which one side, typically business, has the weaponry for policy combat while opponents are entirely disarmed.[5] Lee Drutman has persuasively shown that business, for instance, has a 34–1 advantage in spending on lobbying, up from 22–1 in 1998.[6] One-sided participation, in short, is the rule in American politics, and it is getting worse.

Deliberation requires conflict in order to draw the attention of policymakers and the broader public. When the scope of conflict expands, especially on issues that cut across industries (like tax rates, pollution, and workplace safety), conflict increases, the public becomes enervated, policymakers become concerned about the risks of being too close to concentrated interests, and business does not always win.[7] Such organization is much harder on the kinds of issues we dealt with in previous chapters, which tend to be industry-specific. Without organization of both diffuse as well as concentrated interests, the conflict that is necessary for effective deliberation does not exist. Politicians, even those genuinely concerned for the public interest, may come to believe that there is not in fact any problem to which they need to attend.

Viewing the collective action problem through the lens of deliberation means that we do not have to accept the image of politicians as craven, greedy tools of special interests. Even if all politicians were sincere seekers of the public interest, the collective action problems that inhibit organization of diffuse interests mean that the information that would help politicians to act on the public interest will be unavailable, and the conflict that would draw their attention will be nonexistent.

On top of the advantages enjoyed by all concentrated interests, regressive rent-seekers have another important political asset, namely, their sizable financial assets. Regressive rent-seeking is distinguished by the fact that its beneficiaries are typically quite wealthy. In the case of zoning, we are talking about people in the upper deciles of the income distribution; for finance and intellectual property, people in the top 0.1 percent. Wealth serves as a force multiplier, ensuring not only that people will form organizations to defend their interests but also that they will have more than ample ammunition to expend on political organizing once they do.

The most obvious source of the power of the wealthy is that their financial resources, combined with rent-seekers' concentrated interests, provide an overwhelming motive for political action and substantial means. Those resources can be converted into political power by investing in lobbyists, lawyers, universities, and think tanks. These resources allow the wealthy to dominate the sources of information that policymakers use to understand issues—and to muddy the issue even when the public interest is fairly straightforward. Even if we were to completely eliminate the ability of the wealthy rent-seekers to contribute to political campaigns, their ability to dominate the organizational and informational pathways of influence would give them enormous power.

II SEIZING THE MOMENT

The problems that organizational imbalance pose for democratic decision making are heightened by the "spiky" nature of political activity. Space on the political agenda is always scarce, given the vast activities of contemporary government and limited time and attention of policymakers. That means that the vast majority of issues and problems are not ripe for political decision. What is ripe, meanwhile, is often hard to predict much in advance, with some problems coming onto the agenda suddenly and then dropping off just as quickly.[8]

These moments of agenda focus are particularly important for challengers to rent-seeking because the various sources of power of the wealthy and organized provide only very rare opportunities to expose their extraction to the light of day. When the public is paying attention, many of the advantages of rent-seekers temporarily fall away, as policymakers become fearful of being associated with groups that have gotten an unsavory reputation. Money can buy a degree of policymaker disinterest when the public and the media are not paying attention, but it buys very little when the spotlight shifts.[9]

These moments never last long. Much depends, therefore, on whether the path has been prepared for change even when the odds of action seem long. When a moment of punctuation happens, a great deal depends on whether alternatives to the status quo have been put before the community of relevant policymakers, reducing their uncertainty about the consequences of change. When this kind of vetting has been done, as it was with the deregulation initiatives of the 1970s, huge shifts in policy can happen in moments when the status quo is destabilized.[10] Put another way, we get moments of real deliberation when the advantages of those with stakes in the existing policy environment have deteriorated and the broader public is really paying attention. The quality of government depends a great deal on how well we respond to those moments.

Unfortunately, the organizational imbalance discussed in the previous section has a powerful effect on how governments respond to moments of agenda disruption. If powerful, effective alternatives to the status quo have not been effectively vetted, policymakers may respond by simply cobbling together a bunch of unrelated ideas and presenting it to the public as an appropriate response. That describes a great deal of the politics of Dodd-Frank. There was remarkably little interest-group organization before the financial crisis, and—with the notable and telling exception of Elizabeth Warren's proposal for a consumer financial protection agency—there were few deeply researched and familiar ideas on the shelf.[11] As Mark Schmitt has argued, "No coherent alternative model had been developed, and no effort had been made to build a constit-uency for financial reform. While we had think tanks keep-ing tabs on various aspects of the economy, from the federal budget to the labor market, no one was systematically watching the development of super-complicated financial institutions, noting the risk posed by financial derivatives and promoting alternatives."[12]

An absence of deep organization can assist threatened interests to square the circle of helping policymakers respond to public outrage while protecting them from real policy change. Ilya Somin has shown that this is precisely what most state legislators did in the aftermath of *Kelo v. New London*, when eminent domain abuse suddenly became a huge issue.[13] Armed with substantively empty but superficially responsive legisla-tive alternatives cooked up by lobbyists, policymakers rushed to pass laws that put them on the record as acting on the issue but did not really endanger the ability of large firms to use pub-lic power for private gain. With few organized interests to show that those laws were toothless and to pressure policymakers to enact real change, the moment for change passed with relatively little to show for it.

Even where the wealthy and organized are unable to pre-vent government from responding to a moment of sudden public interest, an absence of effective counter-organizations can help them claw back what they have lost when the spotlight has shifted.[14] While Dodd-Frank was not a particularly coherent or carefully designed piece of legislation, it did have a number of provisions that would have put real pressure on the financial industry. Unfortunately, the overwhelming organizational power of finance has allowed it to throw multiple monkey wrenches into the process of turning the legislation into working regulations. By overwhelming the government in notice-and-comment periods, threatening litigation, and using other tactics, the financial industry has been able to keep the damage from Dodd-Frank to a minimum.[15] This ability to flood the zone of financial policymaking depended on being able to act in every regulatory venue simultaneously, something their opponents could not even remotely match. With every day that decisions were pushed off, the urgency that was present in the immediate aftermath of the financial crisis dimmed, and the pre-crisis power of the financial industry returned.

III INFORMATIONAL BIAS

Modern government is saturated with information. Decisions about whether to go to war, regulate derivatives, invest in infrastructure, tax carbon, and so on are shaped by research that determines what problems policymakers think are worth addressing and makes predictions about the effects that policies will have. The overwhelming majority of policymakers are consumers, rather than producers, of information. Their decisions are determined, in large part, by the information produced by others.

Information is not free. In fact, it is very costly. Consequently, those in a position to produce information that is taken as credible by policymakers have a profound advantage in politics. This is especially true on the myriad questions where politicians' ideological priors do not lead them to an obvious policy response with (as far as they can tell) clear impacts.

Every year, hundreds of millions of dollars are spent on lobbying. Most Americans imagine that these sums are devoted to twisting arms or buying votes. Political scientists have not been friendly to these theories. Instead, they are persuaded by the alternative theory, advanced by Richard Hall and others, that lobbying is a "legislative subsidy," in which legislators and their staff give their time in exchange for the labor and information that lobbyists provide.[16] Legislators want to reduce the risk of unpleasant consequences of their legislative actions, and lobbyists are in a position to provide information that allows them to do so. Something similar is the case for executive branch officials.

A legislative subsidy theory of lobbying also suggests that the less information policymakers are able to collect from sources inside government, the more dependent they become on information from the outside. It is not a surprise, therefore, that the size of the lobbying industry has grown at the same time that the internal capacity of government has been cut (although, of course, that growth has other sources as well).

Lobbying by suppling information may sound more genteel than twisting arms and buying votes, but when spread over the thousands of small decisions that aggregate up into governance, it can produce a powerful bias in policymaking. For instance Cass Sunstein, who served as the head of the White House Office of Information and Regulatory Affairs (OIRA), saw no outright arm-twisting in his time in government. "But if people in the private sector presented arguments, with evidence, about the importance of going in a particular direction, those arguments could matter." This sounds perfectly innocent, except that "those with an incentive to oppose the rules will tend to overstate the costs and perhaps even claim that if rules are finalized, the sky will fall.... If the industry overstates costs, regulators may not have enough information to make a correction."[17] They will not make a correction, to be precise, unless there is a credible source of information on the other side.

As Lee Drutman has argued, this is a far greater power than is typically acknowledged.[18] Policymakers at all levels are fearful of making a terrible mistake that will be traced back to them. Sins of commission, rather than omission, are usually what get people fired or voted out of office.[19] Lobbyists know this, and thus their ability to marshal evidence that a policy change unfavorable to their clients will produce terrible, and traceable, effects, is considerable. It would take considerable information on the other side—for instance, in a complex question about how to regulate a complicated new financial instrument—to combat this informational paralysis. This is where we get back to organizational imbalance, since the capacity to play the information game is so powerfully tilted in the direction of those with the resources to pay for lobbyists. In most of the areas of policy discussed in earlier chapters, that informational subsidy is massively tilted in the direction of the supporters of upward redistribution.

Of course, government itself produces a great deal of information through its substantial investments in official statistics, congressional committees and research organizations, and the offices of policy analysis scattered throughout federal agencies. Those "internal" sources of information could play an important role in providing countervailing information and making it harder for outsiders to effectively claim that a change in policy would cause the sky to fall. Unfortunately, the federal government investment in this capacity has declined considerably over the last 30 years, even as government policies have grown ever more numerous, far-flung, and complicated. This declining capacity has the further effect of making it harder to expand the political agenda by choking off the information that policymakers need to investigate new problems (including problems, such as rent-seeking arrangements, generated by existing policy).[20]

In most policy areas, the political environment is profoundly biased toward those with the resources to invest in information—resources that will be particularly abundant when rents can be recycled into politics. The consequence is that real deliberation, which requires high-quality information on both sides of contested questions, is difficult if not impossible, even if politicians and interest groups have no direct exchange of money.

Informational imbalances have done much to warp policy in all of our case studies. Finance represents an extreme example. After decades of financial innovation, the old simplicity of the "3-6-3 rule" (pay 3 percent on deposits, lend out at 6 percent, get to the golf course by 3) has given way to mind-boggling complexity overseen by "rocket scientists," "quant jocks," and "the smartest guys in the room." To master these complexities requires advanced degrees and years of experience; it is therefore hopeless to expect twenty-something congressional staffers with BAs to be able to keep up with all the technical arcana and see through the weaknesses in the industry's arguments. When the government does attempt to build up its own expertise, it faces the serious problem that individuals with such expertise are paid orders of magnitude more in the private sector than they are on a government payroll. There will always be a challenge, therefore, in attracting well-qualified specialists to government service and ensuring that their analysis is not colored by prospects of a big private-sector payday down the road.

Similar problems afflict policymaking regarding intellectual property. Copyright and patent laws are extremely complex, their intricacies well beyond the understanding of nonspecialists. Likewise, the affected industries, information technology and pharmaceuticals, are high-tech sectors heavily dependent on highly developed human capital. Policymakers are understandably reticent to claim they know better than industry insiders what level of IP protection is best. With both occupational licensing and zoning, the huge mismatches in organizing ability lead to corresponding information imbalances. Professional groups can be expected to supply a surfeit of information on the benefits of licensing, just as homeowner groups can dominate zoning proceedings with chapter and verse on all the potential downsides of new development. Too often there is no one in the room to tell the other side of the story.

IV IMAGE AND AFFLUENCE

The deliberation gap in American politics goes beyond imbalances in information and incentives to participate. Regressive rent-seekers do not rely for their power merely on the brute force of money and organization. They do not go into legislatures and say, "We're rich and we're organized, hand over the loot." And it does not matter that they can produce overwhelming torrents of self-serving information if policymakers don't consider them to be credible sources. To be successful, rent-seekers need to do a convincing job of wrapping their claims in the mantle of the public interest. They need to be able make a persuasive case that, in serving their own interests, they are also making America a wealthier and more just country.

Efforts along these lines are aided immensely by what political scientists call an attractive "policy image."[21] A policy image combines the reputation of the actors who gain from the policy and the public perception of that policy's benefits and costs. When the actors involved have a strong reputation, policymakers will tend to defer to their judgment and be comfortable putting public power in their hands, and will be unlikely to see them as garden-variety grubbers for handouts. When the policy is associated with attractive, widely recognized benefits or attractive symbols, policymakers will be unlikely to probe deeply into its implementation, question the claims made on its behalf, or look for indirect or hidden harms. An attractive policy image leads to policymaker disinterest, a sense that everything is fine, which, more than actual action, is often what rent-seekers are looking for.

Consider occupational licensing. Doctors and dentists do not argue that constraints on market entry are good because they raise their incomes. They argue that licensing is important to protect vulnerable consumers against quacks, or to ensure high levels of professional service. They claim that professionalism is a way to protect against the intrusion of market values on sectors governed by better, higher values. Especially in the case of medicine, they draw on a reputation for serving the public interest; doctors and dentists are generally trusted and not immediately assumed to be acting in their own selfish interest. While the reality of occupational licensing is often the extraction of rents for producers, the image of occupational licensing is professionalism and the protection of consumers.

Intellectual property protection also benefits from a powerful policy image. Entertainment, information technology, and pharmaceutical companies are widely perceived to be ingenious and competitive, powerhouses of creativity and innovation at a time when Americans are anxious about declining dynamism. Advocates for these industries can take advantage of the belief that they represent the "golden eggs" of the American economy, and that it is "pro-business" to protect them. Especially on the left, the fact that this growth does not obviously despoil the environment in the way that manufacturing or extraction does and that industry leaders generally have strongly progressive social views helps burnish the impression that these are businesses the left can support with a clean conscience. Finally, intellectual property protection can draw for conservative support on attractive associations with the concept of "property," even if the concept is problematic when applied to IP.

Although it has deteriorated badly since the crash, the financial sector's policy image was a significant asset in policy disputes during the decades of financialization. The industry featured intimidatingly brilliant "rocket scientists" and "quant jocks" overseen by intimidatingly rich and successful "masters of the universe." Financial innovations pioneered by Nobel Prize winners were incomprehensible to all but a tiny few, but their impressive results were visible for all too see, a huge expansion of access to credit for an increasingly credit-hungry populace. Even now, after the innovative pretensions of finance have been shattered and its capacity for moral bankruptcy has been exposed for all to see, the power of its lobbyists to resist reform remains formidable. Given the US position as a global financial center, any moves to constrain excessive risk-taking can be plausibly portrayed as a direct threat to American competitiveness. With the economy still so weak, those constraints can also be blamed for preventing the resumption of credit expansion and good times.

In any event, the power of finance does not reside in its popularity, for we have long had vivid images of greedy, unscrupulous bankers in our popular culture.[22] Rather, as James Kwak has argued, what matters is the image that finance enjoys among regulators, an image that contributes to what Kwak calls "cultural capture."[23] Regulators have come to identify with the bankers they regulate, seeing them as fundamentally the same people as themselves at different points in their careers, all with a shared objective of protecting the financial industry's interests (even if at some points that may mean sanctioning individual participants).[24] Even more important, Kwak argues, bankers project an image to regulators combining extraordinary wealth, stratospheric intelligence, a belief that that they are essential to economic growth, and work practices supported by the equally high-status discipline of economics. These combine to produce a social status to which financial regulators naturally defer. These elements of cultural capture help explain why financiers can be pilloried by the broad public while still holding powerful sway over the mindset of those tasked with regulating them.

Meanwhile, subsidies for mortgage finance as well as increasingly restrictive land-use regulations benefit from the overwhelmingly positive image of home ownership. Home ownership is associated with family life, roots in the community, and the sturdy bourgeois virtues. Indeed, there is no image more readily associated with the "American dream" than a house with a white picket fence. Any policies that plausibly promise to extend more broadly the blessings of home ownership will thus benefit from enormously powerful emotional associations with love of family and love of country.

In some cases, the power of affluent rent-seekers resides in the fact that their resources allow them to hire lobbyists with networks on both left and right to project different images to the two parties in our polarized system. To conservatives, lobbyists with Republican pedigrees can argue that intellectual property is just another instance of protecting property rights that secure the fruits of individual labor. To liberals, lobbyists with Democratic backgrounds can emphasize IP's association with non-polluting, creative-class economic activity, the part of business Democrats like and that is associated with people they can identify with. Polarization would, perhaps ironically, be enormously helpful to the cause of unwinding excess IP protection, since it would at least ensure that one party was consistently interested in the issue, and make it hard for lobbyists in both parties to work the issue. Defenders of intellectual property have powerful associations that they can make to policymakers on both sides, which prevents Republicans from attacking the policy as crony capitalism and Democrats from savaging it for enriching the advantaged.

Finally, IP, finance, and to some degree occupational licensing are all associated with economic growth and "good jobs." In an era in which high-paying jobs seem to be disappearing, all these sectors claim that they are the cure for what ails. Bankers and IP defenders can also reach out for quasi-mercantilist claims. The financial industry regularly claims that thousands of high-paying jobs would be threatened by regulation, which could send trading to other, less-regulated countries. Supporters of intellectual property argue that software and entertainment are important exports, and American jobs depend on protecting them from uncompensated use.

An especially vivid example of the value of reputation is seen in a column by David Brooks, which cites the following examples of American greatness: "The Food and Drug Administration is the benchmark for medical standards. The American patent system is the most important in the world."[25] The widespread belief that these forms of industry protection are the jewel in the crown of the American economy, rather than an illegitimate profit grab, is an enormous source of social power, and one that means that those industries need to rely far less on more visible, brute-force sources of influence.

The policy image of IP protection is so powerful that in trade negotiations, for instance, industry representatives do not have to lobby in any traditional sense of the term. Their interests are taken as so obviously linked to the national interest that they can operate as partners with the US Trade Representative, safe in the knowledge that what is good for their bottom line is accepted by trade negotiators as their negotiating objective.[26]

Policymakers believe that voters expect them to deliver economic growth, that IP and finance help to do that, and that crackdowns on IP protection, or severe restrictions on banks, would cause traceable, negative effects on employment. This is what Charles Lindblom famously called the "preferential position of business," the fact that negative actions against industry can automatically rebound against policymakers, even in the absence of lobbying.[27] This is magnified in the case of industries believed to be on the frontier of technological progress, since attacks on them can be framed as threatening future prosperity, as well as jobs in the here and now.

Some of the most important rent-seeking interests, like those in finance and IP, are geographically concentrated—finance in New York and Connecticut, information technology in Silicon Valley, entertainment in Los Angeles. For politicians in these areas, supporting the interests of wealthy rent-seekers is not ideological—it is constituent service. While Hillary Clinton and Chuck Schumer were among the most liberal members of the Senate, they also supported Wall Street as strongly as senators for Iowa backed farm subsidies. The same thing can be said about the relationship between very liberal members of Congress from the Bay Area, New York, and Los Angeles. These areas are also where politicians across the country, especially those on the left, go to raise money for political campaigns and public interest groups.[28] Members from those districts are disproportionately able to raise money for other members of Congress, which magnifies their influence over the party's agenda.[29] This does not mean, as some have argued, that the Democratic Party is "owned" by these powerful interests, but it does mean it is cross-pressured. In the politics of upward redistribution, that is often all that is necessary.

Finally, regardless of the varying specific contexts that separate one policy area from another, all regressive rent-seekers benefit from a shared source of favorable policy image. They are all affluent and high-status, and they share common ties and the same cultural milieu with the policymakers who regulate them.

Although rent-seeking is a pervasive feature of democracies, not all rent-seeking schemes are created equal. Taxi drivers in many cities have been able to stymie the entrance of Uber into their markets, reducing competition and increasing their incomes in the process. Whatever one thinks of Uber, and both of us are basically supportive of the business model (if not the scandal-plagued corporate culture), taxi drivers are almost always people of very modest incomes. Labor unions have often been able to increase the wages and job security of their members above what a competitive market would provide, with costs passed on to consumers. But most union members are, at best, middle class.

Our cases feature dynamics that are very distinct from the rent-seeking of taxi drivers and union members. Bluntly put, class matters in the politics of rent-seeking. Class influences rent-seeking through the absence of organizational interest in counteracting its effects. The wealthy have invested in fighting some forms of rent-seeking, as evidenced by the environmental and school reform movements. Given the enormous philanthropic investment in nonprofit policy activity, by contrast, it is quite striking how little money has gone into the areas under investigation in this book. The explanation is simple: these sectors are where a great deal of the money made in the last forty years has come from. No major hedge fund managers are putting their money into organizations that seek to reduce the scale of financialization. None of the great fortunes made in Hollywood or the recording industry have gone into scaling back the protection of copyright law. Given the diffuse interests involved in attacking rent-seeking, an absence of subsidy almost inevitably translates into an absence of countervailing organization.

Class goes beyond mere resources. Affluent rent-seekers can take advantage of social affinities with policymakers that their poorer counterparts cannot. Public officials tend to be disproportionately well educated and thus have common social and educational experiences with those seeking high-end rents.

In fact, as Adam Bonica has found, personal relationships to wealthy donors are particularly important in providing the early money for campaigns—the resources that allow someone to move, for instance, from the state legislature to Congress.[30] In that sense, networks of affluence are part of the invisible primary that initially selects some people for higher offices while passing on others.

Doctors, dentists, car dealers, entertainers, lawyers, and financiers are the friends, neighbors, and business colleagues of policymakers. Even apart from their contributions to their campaigns, these are the sorts of people whom members of Congress and state legislatures see most frequently when they go back to their districts, or who come to their legislative offices. Unlike taxi drivers and union members, these are people whom policymakers know personally. Even before they use their resources to support organized lobbying power, therefore, these groups have a reservoir of common social ties that is a powerful political resource.

V POLICYMAKING IN THE SHADOWS

Rent-seeking seeks out, and thrives in, the shadows. It is most vulnerable when the scope of conflict is the broadest, and strongest where it is the narrowest. Consequently, rent-seekers are more likely to be found in more obscure policy venues where they have special access and where the organizational imbalance we discussed earlier is most pronounced. They are also drawn to institutions where, once they have attained initial success, reversal is maximally difficult.

Occupational licensing is a perfect case of institutional bias. The initial decision to license an occupation, the moment of greatest political vulnerability, is rarely associated with great fanfare. Despite the enormous consequences that the decision will have for the governance of an economic sector, and the difficulty of reversing the decision, there are no special institutional requirements for deliberation or supermajority requirements. Of particular importance, occupational licensing laws are typically quite vague in their scope. The actual consequences of the decision to license are produced by the state licensing boards that determine the conditions for entry to the occupation and the scope of practice. Those boards have members who are, understandably, almost all members of the occupation, as are participants in their meetings. Consequently, their meetings lack genuine deliberation, which requires conflict and enough diversity of participation to force actors to justify their actions in plausible public interest terms. This causes such meetings to take on a quasi-private quality. The line between licensing board and professional association can become very thin indeed.

The decisions that have left our most innovative regions gasping for more housing were similarly made in extremely obscure, low-participation venues. For instance, while the impacts of development restrictions in Silicon Valley are region-wide, the institutions that make them include small-town councils in Menlo Park and Los Altos, both of which have very low rates of political participation. Even in large cities, development decisions are disproportionately influenced by historic preservation commissions with strong biases against new housing. As Edward Glaeser has shown, 16 percent of the buildable land in New York City is in historic districts. In the 1990s those areas "lost an average of 94 housing units (thanks to unit consolidation or conversion to other uses), while the partly historic tracts lost an average of 46 units and the nonhistoric tracts added an average of 89 units."[31]

No area shows the importance of low-profile institutions to the growth of rent-seeking as clearly as intellectual property. Ever since the early 1980s, patent law has been under the exclusive jurisdiction of the US Court of Appeals for the Federal Circuit, which was created with the primary mission of ruling on patent disputes. This institutional shift led to a remarkable increase in pro-patent decisions, and with it the explosion of patents awarded that was discussed in Chapter 4. Because it lacks the cross-pressures of generalist courts, this new court turned out to be unusually susceptible to capture by the patent bar. As Tim Lee of *Vox* argues, "Most obviously, a significant minority of Federal Circuit judges have been patent lawyers themselves, whereas judges on other courts almost never come from a patent law background. Beyond that, the heavy load of patent cases on the court's docket means that the judges of the Federal Circuit are constantly interacting with patent lawyers. In addition to hearing their arguments in the courtroom, they read the same patent law publications as the lawyers, hire young patent lawyers to clerk for them, and are invited to speak at events organized by the patent bar."[32]

Having created a strong pro-patent norm in federal law, protected by an insulated court, the patent bar was then able to lock in those norms through an equally obscure process, international trade law. International trade deals, which are ideologically justified as reducing tariff barriers, are increasingly used to export American law, including IP law, to foreign countries. Driven for decades by the mercantilist, export-promoting politics of the US Trade Representative, these trade deals, once completed, also make it extremely difficult to reevaluate our IP regime. The entry of newer, IP-"dovish" firms like Google has made it harder to expand the IP regime, but its anchoring in a series of low-profile institutions has rendered it highly resistant to reform.

VI WELFARE STATE ON THE CHEAP

Americans do not differ dramatically from the citizens of other advanced industrial countries in what we want from government. Where we do differ is that it is much harder to directly match what government supplies with what citizens demand. Whether it is America's traditional anti-statism, divided government, the parochial tendency of American institutions, or the difficulty politicians have (especially in recent decades) in funding government, all the incentives in American politics push against government's addressing problems in the most direct way possible.[33] And that indirection, it turns out, creates a very leaky bucket of social provision for the wealthy to exploit.

Take, for example, American housing policy. To the degree that there is a genuine social interest in expanding home ownership, there's a very simple way to act on it, a flat matching payment for the down payment on a first home. That would have the advantage of solving the biggest problem that less advantaged home-seekers have (getting the money for a down payment) while also reducing household indebtedness.

Such a direct approach would also be very expensive, so policymakers have understandably looked for more roundabout ways to do the job. They have allowed the deductibility of mortgage interest and deferred capital gains taxes when a home is sold, both of which shower disproportionate benefits on the wealthy while actually making homes more expensive for those out of the market. Even more important, and most relevant to our book, policymakers tried to make home ownership more accessible by, as we showed in Chapter 3, creating elaborate schemes for subsidizing mortgage finance, first through the savings-and-loan industry, and more recently through securitization. Where the leaky bucket of S&Ls dribbled rents to local bankers throughout the United States, mortgage-backed securities concentrated those profits much more tightly, to the smaller group of shadow banking institutions that created them and financiers who traded them.

Similar stories could be told in a multitude of other areas where the same mechanism applies. In the case of finance, for instance, our reliance on 401(k) plans as the backbone of retirement savings generates a large pool of savings for plan administrators and asset managers to skim off while skewing benefits very strongly to the top 20 percent of taxpayers (who get 75 percent of the subsidy).[34] Simply pooling savings into large, indexed accounts (like the federal government's Thrift Savings Plan for its own employees) would liquidate almost all of those financial rents, while reducing the upward redistribution in the program's benefits.

Trying to get a dollar of government for only fifty cents, by "leveraging" the private sector, usually produces very large rents, whether it happens in healthcare, education, pensions, or any of the other areas of the modern welfare state. Despite the fact that those rents generate huge social waste, and in some cases very large risks, the political terrain is biased toward their preservation. Precisely because the rents inevitably generated by these policies are indirect, they are less visible and harder to politicize. Because they are mostly off the books or in the tax code, policy kludges don't read as big government in the same way to conservatives, even though they are often more market-distorting and harder to subject to effective control. While such kludges are rarely the first preference of liberals, they have learned to live with the indirect, leaky approach as the price of having any government response to major social problems.[35]

The combination of all these forces gives wealthy rent-seekers extraordinary advantages in getting what they want from the political system and protecting it once they have it.

The weight of those advantages suggests that upward redistribution cannot be effectively countered simply by well-argued critiques and elegantly designed alternatives. The problem resides in some of the fundamental ways that political power is organized in America, which provide disproportionate advantages to those seeking to enrich themselves at public expense. Reducing upward redistribution, therefore, is fundamentally a problem of diminishing the bias in our political system toward both concentrated interests and those with vast resources.

RENT-PROOFING POLITICS

UPWARD REDISTRIBUTION IS NOT AN accident, and simply making policymakers more aware of its costs and causes cannot reverse it. As Chapter 7 showed, the undertow in the American political process toward upward redistribution is strong, driven by fundamental features of democratic political economy as well as biases that lurk in the specific structures of policymaking. In order to weaken those deep-seated, regressive forces, it will be necessary to rent-proof democracy at multiple levels and across different institutions to generate more egalitarian and pro-innovation outcomes.

What we need is what Madison called a "republican remedy for the diseases most incident to republican government." The essence of our "republican remedies" is more effective, critical deliberation. For deliberation to occur, a number of factors need to be in place. First, there needs to be sufficient public mobilization to bring issues to the attention of policymakers, preventing them from sweeping those problems under the rug or enriching concentrated interests on the sly. Second, there must be enough information on multiple sides so that policymakers can fairly assess the claims before them. Third, policies have to be made in institutional venues that do not give preferential access to the interests of the financially or organizationally advantaged. Institutional and organizational reforms that push policymaking at all levels of government in these directions will make it harder for regressive rent-seekers to get their way and make the policy process more friendly to those who are fighting them.

Our focus is on outlining structural reforms, not detailing ideal policies. In particular, we do not offer the usual laundry list of specific, substantive policy reforms that typically appear in the final chapters of books like this one. It is not our purpose to specify optimal levels of financial regulation, intellectual property protection, occupational screening, or land use controls. On all of these matters, it is clear what we think is the proper direction for policy change: reduced subsidies for excessive risk-taking; narrower scope for and less draconian enforcement of copyrights and patents; lower barriers hindering entry into one's chosen occupation; and less regulatory interference with matching housing supply to demand. As to exactly how far policy change should go, we certainly have our opinions, but we recognize that these are matters on which serious, public-interested citizens can legitimately disagree.

Accordingly, the reform agenda we offer addresses the general contours of policymaking rather than the details of policy outcomes. Our goal is to reorient our institutions so that they do not put such strong pressure on the scale for already advantaged narrow interests. Here are some ways to do it.

I SUBSIDIZE COUNTERVAILING POWER

An organizational imbalance that generates a highly biased information environment for policymaking plays a central role in all the mechanisms of high-end rent-seeking discussed earlier in this book. The empirical claims of those receiving rents are almost always weak, but someone has to actually produce the research and find ways to get the information before policymakers in order to refute those claims. Exposing the weakness of rent-seekers' claims and the naked self-interest behind them is not rocket science, but finding opportunities to do so requires someone to be constantly, carefully building a case and looking out for opportunities. The insulated policymaking venues in which rents are extracted are not, in fact, entirely closed to outsiders, but someone needs to show up at agency rule-making hearings, licensing board deliberations, or city council meetings in which local land-use decisions are made, both to let policymakers know that they are being watched and to get counter-arguments before them. In the absence of such organizational activity, upward redistribution is policymakers' path of least resistance.

Reducing opportunities for rent-seeking requires some workable response to the collective action problem that thwarts the organization of all diffuse interests. The most effective workarounds for this problem in the United States over the last half-century have come through what the political scientist Jack Walker called "third party support," funding from somewhere other than the affected group itself.[1] In the present context, the ironic implication is that efforts to claw back upward-redistributing rents depend significantly on the willingness of wealthy individuals and foundations to provide funding and organization. In other words, it is necessary to check the malignant political influence of the rich and powerful with counter-vailing influence by other elements of the rich and powerful.

Such an approach might seem highly unlikely, but we have ample precedent for wide-ranging philanthropic efforts in the policy arena. Two examples, one on the right and one on the left, are sufficient to show how potent a philanthropically subsidized anti-rent-seeking mobilization could be: first, the environmental movement; and second, the more recent movement toward school reform. Whether or not one agrees or disagrees with the objectives of these two movements, their effectiveness shows that these sorts of investments, when made patiently and sustained over the long term, are able to change the terrain of policy debate, thereby shifting political outcomes. Opponents of regressive regulation, including those with little sympathy for the causes of environmentalism or school reform, have much to learn from both.

Pollution is usefully understood as a form of rent because it represents costs of industrial activity that are not borne by those responsible for them. As a result, polluting activities are more profitable than they would be if costs were internalized. Utilities, chemical producers, mining companies, and other polluters effectively captured government agencies in the years before the institutionalization of the environmental movement, and they possessed a generally positive public image then, too. In fact, "pollution" as a category that incorporated a wide range of environmental harms produced by industrial activity was not a widely recognized problem until the early 1960s.[2]

Donors in the 1960s and '70s, especially the Ford Foundation, poured huge sums into getting a broad range of environmental organizations started.[3] That donor-subsidized, anti-polluter mobilization helped make agency rule-making more pluralistic and repeatedly damaged the reputation of polluters in the public arena. Environmental organizations eventually took root in almost every state, ensuring that polluter interests would no longer enjoy an organizational monopoly in state capitals. Most important, environmental interests were able to use their organization to move policymaking venues from states, where extractive industries had exceptional influence, to the federal government—and within it to the courts and regulatory agencies—where the groups funded by foundations had an organizational advantage.[4]

The engagement of philanthropists was especially vital at the beginning, when political entrepreneurs had not yet identified a constituency willing to support them financially or generated successes that they could leverage to appeal to potential supporters. In the 1960s and 1970s, foundations were willing to step into this breach, getting environmental organizations over this critical initial hump. The result was a correction in the political marketplace that allowed for a surge in environmental regulation, even in relatively challenging times. In fact, foundations were so successful in seeding the environmental organizational landscape that some analysts argue that there may now be too many environmental interest groups for the movement's own good.[5]

Equally potent has been the enormous investment by philanthropists in the cause of education reform over the past two decades. Until recently, as Terry Moe has demonstrated, teachers' unions dominated education policy in most jurisdictions.[6] In most districts, teachers' unions faced no countervailing organization, so they were the only group capable of monitoring officeholders and generating policy alternatives. Teachers had an attractive professional image, which made it easier for them to claim an alignment between their occupational interest, the public interest, and the interests of children. Thousands of localized, specialized institutions like school boards controlled policymaking. While teachers' unions could organize to participate in these relatively obscure venues, what few opponents they had could not. Teachers certainly did not get everything they wanted all the time, but their superior organization and strong image, along with the local venue, gave them a substantial advantage.

In just the past 15 years, the Walton, Gates, Robertson, Arnold, Broad, and Fisher foundations and others have invested large sums of money to increase the number of actors involved in K-12 education policy.[7] Donors have invested heavily in research programs at think tanks like the Brookings Institution and the American Enterprise Institute, making it harder for unions' claims to pass without scrutiny. Foundations have put considerable resources into supporting mayoral control of schools[8] (which has pulled decision making away from teacher-controlled venues like school boards) and charter schools (which move the venue of decision making away from school boards).[9]

Foundations have actively supported litigation, such as the lawsuit *Vergara v. California* brought by the advocacy group Students Matter to challenge protective rules for hiring and firing teachers, the core of teacher union interests.[10] In just the past few years, these same foundations have put millions of dollars into grassroots organizing and lobbying, funding state-based organizations like 50CAN and Stand for Children, parent organizations such as Families for Excellent Schools, leadership pipelines like Leaders for Educational Equity and Students for Education Reform, and the advocacy efforts of charter school operators like Success Academy in New York.[11] This broad range of third-party-supported education-reform organizations has at least partially evened the playing field in education policy, to the point that some observers are starting to worry that it is the reformers who have captured the political system.[12]

Regardless of whether you favor the current approaches to environmental protection or education reform, these examples show that it is possible to create an organized and effective opposition in even deeply entrenched, rent-addled policy areas. They also highlight the scale of the challenge. These two domains are almost certainly the largest and most sustained examples of philanthropic engagement in building an organizational ecology for policy change over the past 50 years.[13] In both cases, foundation interest continued over a long period of time, something that is rarely the case in the philanthropic world. While both initiatives challenged powerful interests, they focused on areas with intrinsic appeal to other wealthy, well-positioned donors.

It will be much harder to find philanthropists with the same zeal for attacking the rents held by doctors, lawyers, financiers, record moguls, and wealthy homeowners. It is not impossible. The wealthy are not a monolith, and it is possible to imagine turning some of them against the ill-gotten gains of others. In some cases, they could act for purely ideological reasons, either egalitarian or free market. In other cases, rent-seeking harms the larger interests of the wealthy themselves. The hypertrophy of patent and copyright law impinges on the interests of many big Internet companies. Sky-high housing prices in the Bay Area also pose real problems for high-tech businesses, including populist backlash against "tech bros" who are blamed for bidding up home values.[14] Many sectors would have a better shot at hiring top talent if the rents from financialization weren't luring away so many of the best and brightest. Throughout corporate America, the challenge of controlling health insurance costs creates incentives to tackle rents in the healthcare sector.

It is not necessary that America's large foundations become convinced of the problem of rent-seeking overall. They must only recognize it in their chosen domain of action. The sheer heterogeneity of America's wealthy is one of the reasons the idea of greater philanthropic attacks on rent-seeking is not a pipe dream. The large fortunes reaped in finance, for instance, do not need to be targeted at the source of philanthropists' own wealth, so long as they are turned against the rents of record companies, pharmaceutical firms, doctors, and lawyers. Philanthropists need to be willing to invest patiently in anti-rent-seeking efforts in precisely the way their counterparts in the environmental and school reform movements did.

II GIVE GOVERNMENT BACK ITS BRAIN

The problem of undue special-interest influence over policy-makers has long been the subject of political reform efforts, but the conventional approach has been to try to disarm the lobby-ists by restricting their use of money to influence elections. An alternative approach is to focus on the other side of the equa-tion, namely, making policymakers resistant to lobbyists' self-serving claims. The best way to do that is to make policymakers less dependent on lobbyists for policy-relevant expertise and information.[15]

American legislative bodies at the federal, state, and local levels have more extensive powers than in other systems, but the staff they rely on in exercising those powers is patronage-riddled, under-qualified, and under-resourced. As a result, the organizational imbalance that favors narrow, well-heeled inter-ests is magnified by the heavy dependence of legislatures on lob-byists for policy-relevant expertise and information. In order to push back against regressive regulation, it is necessary to fortify the internal capacity of legislatures, starting with Congress, to make them capable of real deliberation.

After putting in face time in their districts, overseeing con-stituent services, making yet another round of fundraising calls, and showing up for committee hearings and votes, members of Congress have little time for building up policy expertise and patiently crafting legislation. An army of staff does most of the work needed for actual legislating. Oddly enough, however, it is an army of very young people, chosen largely through patron-age, who hold their positions for a very short time before taking off their Team USA uniforms and going to work for the other side. Without much preexisting subject-matter knowledge, and looking forward to a career in lobbying, young staffers become dependent for information on the interest groups with the resources to provide it.

Even as the ranks of DC lobbyists have exploded in recent decades, Congress's in-house capacity to develop and proc-ess information has declined. Starting around 1980, Congress stopped hiring, then began cutting. House committee staff plunged by almost 40 percent between 1979 and 2005. Today, the Government Accountability Office employs 40 percent fewer staffers than it did in 1979, while staffing at the Congressional Research Service, which provides nonpartisan policy and program analysis to lawmakers, is down 20 percent.[16] The same pattern of diminished in-house expertise can be found throughout government.

There is not much we can do about the size of the lobbyist army trying to influence Congress. Unlike most advocates of political reform, we do not actually think that we have to. Making Congress more deliberative, and less subject to undue influence, is a matter of making it smarter and more independent of the interests trying to bend it to their will. The way to do that, as one of us (Teles) along with Lee Drutman has argued, is to finally bring the civil service system to Congress. To reduce the informational advantage of wealthy rent-seekers, the men and women who whisper in the ears of members of Congress need to be given very different career incentives that keep the best staff from cycling into K Street.

Money is not everything in bullet-proofing congressional staff from undue influence, but it is a start. In personal congressional offices, even staffers in the 90th percentile of salaries earn barely $100,000, while median salaries are consistently below $50,000. Committee staff members earn more, but even those in the 90th percentile are only earning about $160,000, which is what a first-year associate at a Washington law firm makes. Congress doesn't have to pay lobbyist-level salaries, but if we want to keep capacity from seeping out of Congress once the initial burst of idealism confronts the high living costs of Washington, we need to increase salaries, along with creating a generous pension program for senior staff to encourage longevity.

That said, we cannot create a congressional staff system capable of resisting the influence of the rent-seekers just by throwing money at it. If all the additional money went into individual member staff, things might improve a bit but most of the extra resources would be siphoned off into activities that help members get reelected rather than do their job as legislators. Congress needs to concentrate additional resources on top talent in committees, where staffers can focus on developing policy (rather than responding to constituents). The first-best option would be to reconstruct committee staff on the model of the Congressional Budget Office and the Government Accountability Office, which provide stable long-term employment to highly trained policy experts in a context of strict nonpartisanship. Given that most members of Congress are not heads of committees, they are unlikely to centralize and professionalize staff that much.

Short of fully bureaucratizing Congress by putting all resources into its service agencies, we should double committee staff and triple the money available for salaries. Committees would hire all the new staff we are calling for, and the jobs would be merit-based, high-paying positions. Half of the staff would work for the committee, under the direction of whoever is chair. Each congressional member of the committee would have one committee policy staffer detailed to her office on a two-year basis, to help the member with committee issues. Committee staff would go back and forth over time between working exclusively for the committee and working for particular members.

Because the committee would employ individual staffers, their jobs would not depend on whether individual members won or lost their seats. This would free them up to think more about the long-term policy implications instead of being so tied to the electoral fortunes of individual members. By rotating between different members and working solely for the committee, staff would build broader networks, but their core network would remain the committee. This would help to build a strong and lasting community.

A rotation system would keep the job interesting because different potential member bosses would have different priorities and different takes on issues; this would provide staffers new opportunities to learn based on these different areas of focus. An assignment system could be created where staffers and congressional officers jointly rank each other and then get matched based on an algorithm, modeled after the system by which medical students get assigned to residency programs. Here, reputation matters, which means that members and staff who develop a good reputation for quality work will be more likely to get their favored assignments. In such a system, if members repeatedly ranked a staffer as a last choice, that staffer would be fired, preventing the accumulation of dead wood that too often plagues executive branch agencies. This is important because meritocratic systems should have ways of removing the poorest performers.

By tapping into a network of experienced people who know the issues really well, know each other, and have been around, members of Congress will get better policy guidance than they do now from their current staff, who are disproportionately drawn from those who volunteered on their campaign. It would be easier to detect misleading lobbyist arguments. It would also be easier to build support for policies, because the committee staff would all know each other, making it easier for them to work together even across partisan lines.

Enhancing the knowledge that legislatures need to deliberate effectively is particularly vital where highly technical issues like finance and intellectual property are concerned. Precisely because the economic stakes in these areas are so high, overworked and under-trained legislative staff will have a natural tendency to defer to claims by industry representatives that proposed rules will wreck vital areas of the economy, even when those claims lack credibility.[17] Only staff with a great deal of sector-specific knowledge and a high level of technical capacity will have the ability to push back against industry and to bring to their bosses a well-rounded account of the issue. Only an expanded expert staff like this will have the time to drill down into the issues instead of taking the shortcut of deferring to the well-paid lobbyists of the industries they are supposed to be controlling.[18]

III CHANGE THE RULES
OF THE GAME

The strength of high-end rent-seekers emerges over time in a process of accretion. Bit by bit, day after day, countless thousands of individual, small-bore policy choices aggregate up into powerful regressive social outcomes. While we should do what we can to increase the participation of more diffuse rent-seeking opponents and equip government with more tools to resist rent-seekers' special pleading, the logic of collective action still plays very strongly into their hands. The answer, therefore, is to try to tilt the playing board of politics as strongly as possible against regressive regulation, by creating rules that disadvantage the resources that wealthy rent-seekers bring to the table and increase the visibility of funneling more resources to them. It is at the most abstract level of rule-setting that politicians have the strongest incentives to act in the public interest and where disproportionate political mobilization matters the least.

One possible set of changes to the policymaking process would be new forms of central policy clearance. The White House Office of Management and Budget (OMB), for example, performs rigorous central clearance of the federal budget as well as overseeing cost-benefit analysis of regulations through its Office of Information and Regulatory Affairs. OMB is a famously high-status destination for civil servants, attracting some of the best talent from the nation's public policy schools. With its strong reputation and its placement in the White House, OMB has the prestige and power to push back against poorly considered programs or regulations.

The unlikely liberal/libertarian duo of Cass Sunstein and Edward Glaeser has argued for extending central review of regulations to the states, where much of the relevant rent-seeking occurs.[19] Creating 51 state-level Offices of Information and Regulatory Affairs wouldn't be easy, since to serve as more than just a tool of gubernatorial power those offices would need to build the reputation and organizational culture that OMB has taken years to generate. We think this is very much worth the effort.

Critics of process-based regulatory reform argue that this kind of central policy clearance accomplishes little.[20] Because prospective costs and benefits of regulation are necessarily speculative, and retrospective review is beset with serious methodological obstacles, it is always easy to massage the numbers to produce the favored outcome. In other words, politics generally trumps analysis. Although it is true that the analysis provided in policy clearance settings will not overcome settled political opposition, it can aid deliberation by bringing senior policymakers' attention to questions about regulatory effectiveness that otherwise would never have gotten on their radar. When seen as an aid to democratic deliberation rather than a technocratic override, central policy clearance, even with all its limitations, still fulfills an important purpose, especially at the state level where interest-group shenanigans receive so much less scrutiny than they do on issues of national import.

OMB and its counterparts in state government are not the only examples of efficiency-sympathetic agencies that can check their counterparts in other parts of government. The Federal Trade Commission (FTC), for instance, moved in 2010 to charge the North Carolina dental licensing board with antitrust violations for trying to clamp down on unlicensed teeth whitening clinics, and the FTC's action was upheld by the Supreme Court in 2014.[21] Since the Supreme Court decision, the FTC is now providing guidance to state authorities on the federal antitrust implications of their licensing policies. Consequently, if an anti-rent organization in a state can generate enough energy to get a state legislator to request the FTC to issue an advisory opinion, it can introduce a very powerful, highly authoritative counterweight into a normally insulated and imbalanced decision-making process. The FTC could be doing even more in this area by providing more resources to pay for research and participate in state deliberations. The FTC could also be given a greater voice on federal regulations with impacts on competition, to complement OMB's existing cost-benefit review.[22] These changes would make regulatory decisions more deliberative by introducing a wider range of authoritative voices into agency decision making, especially voices without long-standing relationships with regulated firms.

In addition to expanding the oversight activities of existing agencies, new bodies could provide authoritative analysis of rent-creating policies. To tackle the governance problems that afflict financial regulation, the economist Ross Levine has proposed the creation of a special Financial Regulatory Commission, also known as "the Sentinel," whose sole job would be to prepare an annual report to Congress on the quality and effectiveness of regulation in light of changing market conditions. The president and Senate would confirm members; moreover, commission members would be prohibited from receiving compensation from the financial industry after their terms expire. Levine's argument "is that no other existing entity currently has the incentives, power, or capabilities to perform the FRC's role as a public sentinel over the full constellation of financial sector policies."[23]

One could easily imagine a valuable role for a similar federal commission charged with reviewing intellectual property law. Here, the commission might exist only for a fixed term, and its job would be to provide a comprehensive review of how specific provisions of patent and copyright law encourage or deter artistic creation and technological innovation. No authoritative evaluation of the whole of IP policy—from patent and copyright terms to the criteria for patentability to the scope of fair use and on and on—has ever been conducted to assess how well or how poorly current policy fulfills the constitutional mandate to improve science and the useful arts. Such a report by commissioners with a reputation both for subject-matter expertise and impartiality would be an important resource for IP reformers seeking to roll back misguided expansions of patent and copyright protection.

As valuable as this sort of efficiency-based central review is, it leaves out entirely the distributive dimension of public policy. As part of its central review of regulations, OMB (and its future counterparts at the state level) could conduct some form of distributive analysis whenever it determines that a new regulation is creating rents via subsidies or entry barriers. Such an analysis would highlight cases where new rules simultaneously reduce efficiency and enrich already wealthy interests.[24] Congress could likewise require that the CBO undertake a distributive analysis of major legislation whenever new subsidies are conferred. Such reviews would not prevent upward redistribution through the regulatory and legislative process, but they would sharpen deliberation by forcing politicians to openly approve of rent-seeking schemes. Also, they would subsidize the efforts of outside advocacy organizations by taking very expensive analytical work off their plate and putting issues onto the agenda of legislators.

Another way to reduce rent-seekers' advantages in the lobbying game is to move to a different playing field. Rent-seekers typically prefer relatively low-profile, obscure venues where their specialized knowledge and resources allow them to operate much more effectively than their potential opponents. For comparison's sake, consider how important it was for education reformers to move schooling governance from special purpose institutions (school boards) that were easily captured by teacher unions to mayoral control.[25] This move disadvantaged the kinds of resources that teacher unions possess, while advantaging those of reformers.

The parallels with some of our cases are striking. The dysfunctions of land-use regulation are to a significant degree an artifact of the policymaking venue and process. Decisions are made at the local level, where parochial interests are relatively strongest; further, they are typically made parcel by parcel, further magnifying the influence of NIMBY (not in my backyard) opposition to development. In addition to ordinary zoning, land use is further restricted by highly insulated institutions like historical preservation commissions that are easily captured by anti-development forces.

Accordingly, progress in reversing the trend toward evergreater restrictiveness in land use would be greatly aided by changes in where and how decisions are made. David Schleicher of Yale Law School, for example, has proposed the idea of a municipal zoning budget. Under such a scheme, the city government would decide every year on a target for how much the overall housing stock should increase. Until the target is reached, so-called downzonings that impose additional restrictions on parcels of land would be disallowed; after the target is reached, any downzonings would have to be balanced by offsetting rezonings that reduce restrictions elsewhere.[26] Along similar lines, Edward Glaeser has advocated use of historic preservation budgets to impose needed discipline on this increasingly popular form of land-use regulation.[27] Even more boldly, Glaeser has called for moving control over land use away from localities entirely and vesting it with state authorities who have a broader perspective on the benefits as well as costs of development. The state would write its own code for building, including perhaps specifying impact fees to pay off negatively affected neighbors; localities could decide to be more permissive than the state code, but not more restrictive.[28]

Changing the policymaking venue is especially important to resisting and rolling back rent-seeking in intellectual property law. One promising reform would be to eliminate the exclusive jurisdiction of the US Court of Appeals for the Federal Circuit over patent cases. No less an authority than chief judge for the Seventh Circuit Diane Wood has argued for this reform.[29] Such a move would create a more deliberative context for policymaking, not only by forcing the CAFC to look over its shoulder at courts less institutionally sympathetic to patents but also by increasing the alternative opinions available to the Supreme Court on appeal.

The incorporation of intellectual property provisions in trade agreements has had an especially baleful influence over policy. First, those agreements have allowed the United States to export its flawed IP model to countries around the world. Second, by locking in important elements of the US policy status quo as international commitments, trade agreements have created formidable obstacles to improving US law. Much damage has already been done, but at least we can stop digging the hole deeper: the inclusion of rent-creating IP provisions in future trade agreements should be stoutly resisted. One possible means to this end would be to amend congressional grants of trade promotion authority (which commits Congress to an up-or-down vote on agreements without any amendments) to exclude IP provisions from "fast track" consideration.

Finally, we should at least consider the possibility that Congress, and legislatures in general, is unavoidably tilted toward upward redistribution. William Howell and Terry Moe have recently argued that Congress is systematically biased toward narrow, provincial interests and that the presidency, regardless of whose hands it is in, is more open to efficiency-based arguments.[30] Howell and Moe suggest that the best way to counter Congress's rent-friendly provincialism is to require Congress to give an up-or-down vote to legislation proposed by the president. In other words, Congress must "fast track" consideration not just for trade agreements but for domestic legislation as well. This admittedly dramatic procedural reform would give presidents much more power to shape the policy alternatives considered by Congress. Greater White House control over the policy agenda would in turn lead Congress to focus on what it is best at, deliberating on the general merits of legislation, while minimizing its tendency to build majorities by handing out favors to concentrated interests.

IV EGALITARIAN LOCHNERISM?

Restructuring policymaking processes in both the legislative and executive branches is needed to reduce rent-seeking, but it is not enough. Any serious attack on upward-redistributing rents will need to enlist the power of the judiciary, especially to take on policies at the state and local level. The sheer number of licensing and land-use restrictions in place over thousands of jurisdictions nationwide is more than even a well-resourced anti-rent organizational network could effectively challenge directly. These restrictions are so pervasive and deeply ingrained that the political branches may never be able to root them out. Some institutional counterbalance in the form of judicial review is required.

Least controversially, the judiciary can push back against rent-seeking through statutory interpretation. This possibility is especially attractive in the case of intellectual property, since a great deal of existing copyright and patent policy consists of judge-made law. What judges made, they are free to unmake. A concerted effort to educate judges on the dysfunctions of current law, along the lines of the famous law-and-economics seminars organized by Henry G. Manne, could yield fruit down the road in the form of new doctrines that better reconcile the realities of copyright and patent laws with their supposedly animating objectives.[31]

Occupational licensing is another area in which changes in statutory construction could buoy the efforts of anti-rent reformers. Specifically, the "state action" doctrine under which state licensing boards claim antitrust immunity is a judge-made creation. The Supreme Court has already ruled that there is no blanket immunity for licensing boards in its 2014 decision in *North Carolina Board of Dental Examiners v. Federal Trade Commission*, but the bounds of immunity remain unclear.[32] A clarifying ruling that narrows the scope of the state action doctrine would likewise narrow the capacity of licensing boards to engage in anticompetitive mischief.

The Supreme Court's decision in *North Carolina Dental Examiners* shows how the judiciary can nudge democratic decision making toward being more deliberative. The Court ruled that the North Carolina licensing board had to be meaningfully overseen by elected officials if it was to preserve its antitrust immunity. By putting every state in the country on notice that its licensing decisions are vulnerable to attack on antitrust grounds, the decision enhances democratic deliberation in three ways. First, it encourages states to take a second look at licensing arrangements that legislatures are never asked to reconsider. Second, by insisting that boards have meaningful political oversight, the decision could lead elected officials to take seriously that licensing boards represent public authority, exercising coercion, and are not just benign forms of professional self-governance. Third, by granting less deference to boards that are dominated by the profession they regulate, it could encourage states to appoint less-captured boards, which would foster greater deliberation through a wider range of opinions.

A much more controversial use of judicial power would be to strike down rent-creating regulations on constitutional grounds. Here the judicial role is not to encourage more deliberative democracy but to offer an escape hatch from dysfunctional democratic outcomes when deliberation has failed to prevent them. Since the 1930s, however, judicial review of economic regulation has been all but a dead letter. Under prevailing precedents, such regulation is deemed constitutional so long as it is "rationally related" to a legitimate state purpose, and the standards for determining rationality have been extremely lax. The Supreme Court's quietism has been deemed necessary to avoid a return to the "Lochner era," when the Court regularly struck down state and federal regulations.

Nevertheless, thanks to a 2013 decision by the Fifth Circuit Court of Appeals, the constitutionality of at least some occupational licensing laws is now in question. Under Louisiana law, only licensed funeral directors could sell caskets to the public. A Benedictine abbey that sought to sell simple, inexpensive wooden caskets challenged the law, and the Fifth Circuit found in the monks' favor. Although it still applied the accommodating "rational basis" standard, the Fifth Circuit held that protecting a domestic industry from competition did not constitute a legitimate state interest and that the restriction on casket sales was not rationally related to legitimate state interests in consumer protection or public health and safety.[33] But in 2004, in a similar case involving Oklahoma's regulation of casket sales, the Tenth Circuit Court of Appeals ruled differently, finding that economic protectionism is "the favored pastime of state and local government" and thus a legitimate state interest.[34] Given this clear conflict between the circuits, the Supreme Court could weigh in to resolve the matter. If the Court were to do so and side with the Fifth Circuit, constitutional challenges to occupational licensing laws on economic liberty grounds could become much more common.

Progressives would surely denounce such a development, but their reasons for doing so are less than ironclad. The usual basis for denouncing "Lochnerism" is that it is illegitimate for unelected judges to act as a super-legislature and strike down laws passed by democratically elected representatives. However, on abortion and single-sex marriage, among other issues, progressives praise the Court for second-guessing the results of representative democracy, even though the textual basis in the Constitution for these interventions is hardly clear. The great fear of judicial review in the economic arena is that, with no clear analytical lines to limit judicial discretion, it could metastasize into a full-fledged assault on the modern regulatory state. That is a serious concern. Yet it is at least possible to imagine a middle ground between today's complete deference and free-wheeling Lochnerian activism, one in which judicial review serves not to undermine the regulatory state but to safeguard its hygiene by targeting only baldly protectionist and anticompetitive rent-seeking.

A somewhat less fraught possibility is that occupational licensing and similar protectionist regulations could be struck down under state constitutional law. In 2015, for example, the Texas Supreme Court ruled against state efforts to crack down on eyebrow threading boutiques for the unlicensed practice of cosmetology. Obtaining a Texas cosmetology license required 750 hours of training, over 300 of which were conceded by the state to be completely irrelevant to eyebrow threading. These extraneous requirements were deemed by the Court to be so "oppressive" as to violate the state constitution's due process clause.[35] The same fears of a revived Lochnerism are present here, but at least the scope is restricted. Ongoing experimentation at the state level might reveal whether a sustainable middle ground can be found for judicial review of economic regulation. Given the tendency of state supreme courts to follow the federal lead on interpretation of analogous constitutional provisions, we expect such experiments to be rare.

The most promising basis for judicial review of rent-creating regulations lies not in ideologically polarizing expansions of constitutional law but in novel applications of administrative law. Legal scholar John Blevins has proposed using three different standards of review, depending on the provenance of the restriction in question. For municipal regulations (such as those covering taxis and ridesharing, AirBnB, and food trucks), he recommends "hard look" review under the "arbitrary and capricious" standard used in cases under the Administrative Procedures Act; since municipalities derive their powers from the state, their regulations can be considered analogous to agency actions. For state agency interpretations of licensing laws (e.g., a determination of whether eyebrow threading constitutes the practice of cosmetology), Blevins calls for application of a "clear statement" rule in which agency interpretations that extend licensing requirements to any activity not explicitly contemplated by the underlying statute would be rejected by the courts. In the third case, when the statute expressly imposes a licensing restriction, courts should defer to the will of the legislature. Blevins's approach, then, avoids any direct overruling of clear legislative action while creating opportunities for meaningful scrutiny of licensing restrictions when the legislature has not spoken directly on point.[36]

One of the most important mechanisms by which occupational licensing expands is through the insidious, incremental expansion of its jurisdiction by licensing boards controlled by occupational insiders. In fact, once the legislature has created a licensing scheme and structured a board in such a way that it can be controlled by the licensed profession, such incremental expansion is all but inevitable. Courts can play a useful role in preventing the gradual growth of licensing by applying a very narrow interpretation of licensing restrictions rather than deferring to licensing boards. If a licensing board wanted to expand the scope of its jurisdiction, it would have to go back to the legislature to get fresh legal authority to do so. This would switch the institutional bias of the licensing system. Where now licensing advocates get most of what they want unless opponents can mobilize an unusual amount of pushback, with a narrow interpretation of their authority, all opponents need to do is prevent legislative action from occurring. Once again, such a change would be pro-deliberative, in that it would force advocates of licensing to openly present their arguments and generate a legislative coalition rather than being able to rely on institutional inertia.

V LIBERALTARIAN POLITICS

The politics of an anti-rent reform agenda cut defiantly across the usual ideological and partisan divisions. Of the four case studies we examined, only with respect to financial regulation do we see the usual left-right debate of bigger versus smaller government. Even here there are important intra-party tensions, as the more ideologically minded on both the left and the right decry the cozy relationships between the centrist bipartisan establishment and Big Finance and the favoritism and bailouts that ensue.[37]

For the other policy areas we examine, the opposing forces have little ideological or partisan coherence. Accordingly, champions of pro-growth, egalitarian reform are found on both sides of the aisle. In the field of intellectual property, for example, Nancy Pelosi (D-CA) joined forces with Darrell Issa (R-CA) and Ron Paul (R-TX) to oppose the Stop Online Piracy Act, a failed legislative effort to toughen criminal penalties for copyright violations. Until relatively recently, concern over the excesses of occupational licensing and zoning was restricted to a tiny handful of libertarian economists, but strongly pro-market position papers under the Obama administration on both issues highlight the growing progressive interest in reform on these fronts.[38]

Attacking upward redistribution is a cross-party project; alas, we live in an extremely partisan time. Party polarization has also driven institutional gridlock, in which big reforms of the kind that we suggest have become hard to push through while small manipulations of the rules are the name of the game. Many important attacks on rent-seeking in the past drew on cross-party coalitions of reformers mobilized against entrenched interests,[39] but it is much harder to build such coalitions than in the past. Is the political window for "liberaltarian" reforms closed?[40] Is it impossible to build an effective political coalition for political reforms that will produce a more competitive, egalitarian economy?

No one can know the future, but we think there is a good chance that the next couple of decades will look very different from the last. In recent times, the economic policy battle lines have been very clear, with the agenda dominated by questions of the size of government, including higher or lower taxes and more or less social provision. On these issues, the parties are increasingly homogeneous. When the parties are as coherent as they are now, members are willing to transfer power to their leaders, whose incentive is to place issues on the agenda that their members agree on and keep off the agenda those few issues where they do not. There is little opportunity for cross-party cooperation, but until recently there has also been very little interest either.

The recent past may not be prologue. The 2016 presidential campaign revealed massive fault lines running through both major parties. In the wake of the Sanders and Trump candidacies, both parties now confront an insurgent populism that seeks a decisive break with establishment orthodoxy. How these confrontations will resolve remains anybody's guess, but it is entirely possible that major partisan realignments are in the offing. While the fur is flying, issues that split the parties rather than unite them will likely enjoy greater prominence. The longer this unsettled state of affairs continues, and the more party-scrambling issues rise up the agenda of ordinary working politicians, the more those politicians will want institutional rules that make it easier for them to reach across the aisle to cut deals.

What happens when the preferences of members shift in this way? Conditional party government theory in political science, backed by history, suggests that institutional rules will change.[41] Members will be less willing to transfer power to their leaders, and they will want that power sent back to committees where deals can be more easily struck. When coalitions cannot find a home in the committees, members will want rules that let them go around the institutional structure of Congress entirely. Congress and state legislatures could go back to the more entrepreneurial structure that they had in the 1970s, in which individual members have more freedom to put together strange-bedfellows coalitions based on temporary alignments across ideological lines.

Such coalitions don't necessarily require a less ideological Congress. Indeed, the progress of ideological purism, whether of the anti-statist or egalitarian variety, can facilitate new political groupings. Consider, for example, criminal justice reform, where many conservatives have become more skeptical of mass incarceration precisely because they have gone further in an anti-statist direction.[42] Something similar can occur with respect to finance and intellectual property, where anti-statism has led some conservatives to see crony capitalism where once they saw support for business. Ideological purists on both poles may find more friends at the other extreme than they can cobble together on their own team.

With the parties in Congress weakened, the incentives for outside actors to encourage strange-bedfellows coalitions would increase. Interest groups would develop more of the skills needed to build relationships and trust between dyed-in-the-wool liberals and conservatives. Think tanks would shift their agenda to emphasize developing the informational base for transpartisan coalitions. Legislators in Congress, in turn, would be able to draw on this supply of policy ideas to assemble cross-party legislative coalitions. Such developments would create a virtuous cycle of increasing both demand for transpartisan policy ideas as well as the available supply.

That does not mean that the major differences over the scope of state action that have divided the parties will disappear. What it does mean is that the near-disappearance of strange-bedfellows coalitions on big, national-level policy will abate.

This is all relevant to the agenda of this book, because the ideological space for transpartisan reform is almost exclusively liberaltarian.[43] While Democrats and Republicans could once agree on expansions of state activity so long as the mechanism was business-friendly (think for instance of Medicare Part D), there's next to no chance of Republicans joining such a coalition today. Where more ambitious policy change is concerned, the point of convergence is where anti-statism and egalitarianism meet.

The effort by each party to push the boundaries of state action back and forth will not disappear. So long as our institutional constraints remain more or less what they are today, the opportunities for doing so, as in the brief moment of overwhelming Democratic control in 2009–10, will be rare. We have gotten used to the idea that nothing important can happen in the long interim periods in which the parties are sharing control. In the world we envision, the weakening of party control and the shift in the larger policy agenda could render these periods of joint party control highly productive rather than gridlocked.

There are big things that need to happen in order to address the twin evils of sluggish growth and inequality that cannot attract transpartisan coalitions, and progress on those fronts will have to await the rare moments of unified government control. It is not necessary for us to sit on our hands while we wait. Here we have laid out an ambitious agenda of policy and institutional reform whose natural coalition cuts right across the parties and whose most logical supporters are each party's most strident members.

It is possible, in other words, to attack the crisis of governance that has threatened our constitutional government with both partisan and transpartisan approaches. The parties can continue to wage the economic fight they've had for 40 years on taxing and spending while our political system makes room for a parallel conflict between the forces of upward redistribution and those of competitive egalitarianism.

The need for liberaltarian politics has never been greater. Populism, authoritarianism, crony capitalism, and ethnonationalism are on the march, not only in the United States but across Europe as well. Liberalism, meanwhile, is on its heels. After the heady triumphalism of the "end of history" years, the future vitality of liberal democratic capitalism—in the United States, in Europe, and across the world—is now open to serious question. If that vitality is to be restored and maintained, liberalism must show that it can once again be a genuine fighting faith rather than an anemic justification for the status quo.

In particular, liberal politics must demonstrate that it is up to the job of generating fairer, faster growth. Rising to that challenge will require liberals of all parties to think anew, reconsidering older commitments and opening themselves up to new kinds of coalitions. The time to do so, sadly, may be shorter than we think.

NOTES

Chapter 1

1. Raj Chetty, David Grusky, Maximilian Hell, Nathaniel Hendren, Robert Manduca, and Jimmy Narang, "The Fading American Dream: Trends in Absolute Mobility since 1940," National Bureau of Economic Research Working Paper no. 22910, December 2016, http://www.nber.org/papers/w22910; Alex Johnson, "Exit Polls: NBC News' Analysis of 2016 Votes and Voters," November 9, 2016, http://www.nbcnews.com/storyline/2016-election-day/election-polls-nbc-news-analysis-2016-votes-voters-n680466.
2. See Thomas Piketty and Emmanuel Saez, "Income Inequality in the United States, 1913–1998," *Quarterly Journal of Economics* 118, no. 1 (February 2003): 1–39, http://piketty.pse.ens.fr/fichiers/public/PikettySaez2003.pdf; World Wealth and Income Database, http://www.wid.world/.
3. We recognize the likelihood that a continuing shortfall in demand since the Great Recession may also be contributing to slow growth.
4. One of us has written extensively on the US growth slowdown. See Brink Lindsey, "Why Growth Is Getting Harder," Cato Institute Policy Analysis no. 737, October 8, 2013, http://www.cato.org/publications/policy-analysis/why-growth-getting-harder; Brink

Lindsey, "Low-Hanging Fruit Guarded by Dragons: Reforming Regressive Regulation to Boost U.S. Economic Growth," Cato Institute white paper, 2015, http://www.cato.org/publications/white-paper/low-hanging-fruit-guarded-dragons-reforming-regressive-regulation-boost-us; Brink Lindsey, ed., *Understanding the Growth Slowdown* (Washington, DC: Cato Institute, 2015).

5. See, e.g., Manuel Funke, Moritz Schularick, and Christoph Trebisch, "Going to Extremes: Politics after Financial Crises, 1870–2014, Centre for Economic Policy Research Discussion Paper no. 10884, October 2015, http://cepr.org/active/publications/discussion_papers/dp.php?dpno=10884; Amy R. Krosch and David M. Amodio, "Economic Scarcity Alters the Perception of Race," *Proceedings of the National Academy of Sciences of the United States of America* 111, no. 25 (June 24, 2014): 9079–84, http://www.pnas.org/content/111/25/9079.full.pdf (negative perceptions of racial minorities accentuated under conditions of economic scarcity); Lincoln Quillian, "Prejudice as a Response to Perceived Group Threat: Population Composition and Anti-Immigrant and Racial Prejudice in Europe," *American Sociological Review* 60, no. 4 (August 1995): 586–611 (racial prejudice a function of economic conditions and size of minority group relative to dominant group).

6. Benjamin Friedman, *The Moral Consequences of Economic Growth* (New York: Knopf, 2005), p. 4.

7. See Kevin Drum, "Economic Anxiety Is All about Progress, Not Income," *Mother Jones*, August 23, 2016, http://www.motherjones.com/kevin-drum/2016/08/economic-anxiety-all-about-progress-not-income.

8. See Jonathan T. Rothwell, "Explaining Nationalist Political Views: The Case of Donald Trump," draft working paper, September 4, 2016, http://papers.ssrn.com/sol3/papers.cfm?abstract_id=2822059.

9. Arthur Okun, *Equality and Efficiency: The Big Tradeoff* (Washington, DC: Brookings Institution, 1975).

10. See Daniel Carpenter and David A. Moss, *Preventing Regulatory Capture: Special Interest Influence and How to Limit It* (New York: Cambridge University Press, 2014).

11. See, e.g., N. Gregory Mankiw, "Defending the One Percent," *Journal of Economic Perspectives* 27, no. 3 (Summer 2013): 21–34, https://www.aeaweb.org/articles?id=10.1257/jep.27.3.21.

12. See Thomas Piketty, *Capital in the Twenty-First Century* (Cambridge, MA: Belknap Press, 2014).
13. Barry Goldwater, *The Conscience of a Conservative* (New York: MacFadden Books, 1960), p. 23.
14. Interview on National Public Radio, *Morning Edition*, May 25, 2001.
15. Anna Persson and Bo Rothstein, "It's My Money: Why Big Government Is Good Government," *Comparative Political Studies* 47, no. 2 (January 2015): 231–49.
16. Joseph Stiglitz, Nell Abernathy, Adam Hersh, Susan Holmber, and Mike Konczal, "Rewriting the Rules of the American Economy," http://rooseveltinstitute.org/rewriting-rules-report/.
17. Frank Levy and Peter Temin, "Inequality and Institutions in 20th Century America," SSRN Working Paper 07-17, June 27, 2007.
18. The connection between excessive governmental informalism and capture by the organized was recognized on the left as far back as Theodore Lowi's great book, *The End of Liberalism* (New York: W. W. Norton, 1979).
19. Joseph E. Stiglitz, *The Great Divide: Unequal Societies and What We Can Do about Them* (New York: W. W. Norton, 2016); Joseph E. Stiglitz, *The Price of Inequality: How Today's Divided Society Endangers Our Future* (New York: W. W. Norton, 2013).
20. Jason Furman and Peter Orszag, "A Firm-Level Perspective on the Role of Rents in the Rise of Inequality," presentation at "A Just Society" Centennial Event in Honor of Joseph Stiglitz, Columbia University, New York, October 16, 2015, https://obamawhitehouse. archives.gov/sites/default/files/page/files/20151016_firm_level_ perspective_on_role_of_rents_in_inequality.pdf.
21. See, e.g., Dean Baker, *Rigged: How Globalization and the Rules of the Modern Economy Were Structured to Make the Rich Richer* (Washington, DC: Center for Economic and Policy Research, 2016)
22. See Luigi Zingales, *A Capitalism for the People: Recapturing the Lost Genius of American Prosperity* (New York: Basic Books, 2012).
23. See the Stigler Center's website at https://research.chicagobooth. edu/stigler.
24. Barry Lynn, *Cornered: The New Monopoly Capitalism and the Economics of Destruction* (New York: Wiley, 2010)

25. Stuart Hampshire, *Justice Is Conflict* (Princeton, NJ: Princeton University Press, 2001).
26. Frank Baumgartner et al., *Lobbying and Policy Change: Who Wins, Who Loses, and Why* (Chicago: University of Chicago Press, 2009).
27. Suzanne Mettler, *The Submerged State: How Invisible Government Policies Undermine American Democracy* (Chicago: University of Chicago Press, 2011).

Chapter 2

1. Rents can also arise from an increase in industrial concentration. These rents can be natural, artificial, or something in between. For the first, think of pro-consumer exploitation of scale economies; for the second, think anticompetitive collusion; for the third, think mergers. We discuss this phenomenon later in this chapter.
2. See Owen Zidar, "Corporate Profits as a Share of GDP," *owenzidar* (blog), May 6, 2013, https://owenzidar.wordpress.com/2013/05/06/corporate-profits-as-a-share-of-gdp/.
3. Jason Furman and Peter Orszag, "A Firm-Level Perspective on the Role of Rents in the Rise of Inequality," presentation at "A Just Society" Centennial Event in Honor of Joseph Stiglitz, Columbia University, New York, October 16, 2015, https://obamawhitehouse.archives.gov/sites/default/files/page/files/20151016_firm_level_perspective_on_role_of_rents_in_inequality.pdf.
4. Furman and Orszag, "A Firm-Level Perspective on the Role of Rents in the Rise of Inequality."
5. James Bessen, "Accounting for Rising Corporate Profits: Intangibles or Regulatory Rents?" Boston University School of Law, Law & Economics Working Paper no. 16–18, May 11, 2016, https://www.bu.edu/law/files/2016/05/Accounting-for-Rising-Corporate-Profits.pdf.
6. See Council of Economic Advisers, "Benefits of Competition and Indicators of Market Power," updated May 2016, https://obamawhitehouse.archives.gov/sites/default/files/page/files/20160414_cea_competition_issue_brief.pdf.

7. An argument that consolidation is, in fact, bad for growth can be found in Mike Konczal and Marshall Steinbaum, "Declining Entrepreneurship, Labor Mobility and Business Dynamism," Roosevelt Institute Paper, http://rooseveltinstitute.org/declining-entrepreneurship-labor-mobility-and-business-dynamism/.

8. The concept of contestable markets comes from William Baumol, John Panzar, and Robert Willig, *Contestable Markets and the Theory of Industry Structure* (New York: Harcourt, Brace and Jovanovich, 1982).

9. See Ryan Decker, John Haltiwanger, Ron Jarmin, and Javier Miranda, "The Role of Entrepreneurship in U.S. Job Creation and Economic Dynamism," *Journal of Economic Perspectives* 28, no. 3 (Summer 2014): 3–24; Ryan Decker, John Haltiwanger, Ron Jarmin, and Javier Miranda, "The Secular Decline in Business Dynamism in the U.S.," unpublished manuscript, June 2014, http://econweb.umd.edu/~haltiwan/DHJM_6_2_2014.pdf; E. J. Reedy and Robert E. Litan, "Starting Smaller; Staying Smaller: America's Slow Leak in Job Creation," Kauffman Foundation Research Series: Firm Formation and Economic Growth, July 2011.

10. See John Haltiwanger, "Business Dynamism and Growth," in Brink Lindsey, ed., *Understanding the Growth Slowdown* (Washington, DC: Cato Institute, 2015).

11. The assumption is heroic but defensible. It is true that regulation can reduce rents by internalizing externalities (e.g., pollution) or addressing other market failures. On the other hand, even when regulations are aimed appropriately at addressing genuine market failures, they can still act as entry barriers—and thereby create rents—as an unintended side effect. Regulatory compliance typically entails fixed costs that don't vary with firm size, which means they give a competitive advantage to bigger, older firms that can spread those costs over much larger operations.

12. See Omar Al-Ubaydli and Patrick A. McLaughlin, "RegData: A Numerical Database on Industry-Specific Regulations for All United States Industries and Federal Regulations, 1997–2012," *Regulation & Governance*, 2015, doi: 10.1111/rego.12107.

13. In addition to the obvious limitations of such a methodology, RegData is further limited by its exclusive focus on federal

regulation. As our book will show, some of the most damaging regulatory rents are being created at the state and local level.

14. See Bessen, "Accounting for Rising Corporate Profits." The RegData index has also been used to test the effect of regulation on new business formation, with conflicting results. James Bailey and Diana Thomas of Creighton University found a statistically significant relationship between increasing regulatory restrictiveness and lower rates for both start-ups and firm employment growth. James Bailey and Diana Thomas, "Regulating Away Competition: The Effect of Regulation on Entrepreneurship and Employment," Mercatus Working Paper, September 2015, http://mercatus.org/publication/regulating-away-competition-effect-regulation-entrepreneurship-and-employment. On the other hand, Alex Tabarrok of George Mason University and Nathan Goldschlag of the Census Bureau compared regulatory intensity across industries but were unable to find a negative effect of regulations on dynamism. Instead, they found that more heavily regulated industries actually had higher start-up and hiring rates. Alex Tabarrok and Nathan Goldschlag, "Is Entrepreneurship in Decline?" in *Understanding the Growth Slowdown*, ed. Brink Lindsey (Washington, DC: Cato Institute, 2015).

15. Growth can also be boosted temporarily by increasing the amount of inputs used in production. But once the increase in inputs stops, the level of output will eventually stabilize and thus the growth rate will subside. And any increase in inputs will stop sooner or later because of the law of diminishing returns. At some point, the marginal product of one more worker or one more piece of equipment will equal its marginal cost, at which point no net addition to output occurs.

16. See John Haltiwanger, "Job Creation and Firm Dynamics in the United States," in *Innovation Policy and the Economy*, ed. Josh Lerner and Scott Stern, vol. 12 (Chicago: University of Chicago Press, 2012), pp. 17–38.

17. Lucia Foster, John Haltiwanger, and C. J. Krizan, "Aggregate Productivity Growth: Lessons from Microeconomic Evidence," in *New Directions in Productivity Analysis*, ed. Edward Dean,

Michael Harper, and Charles Hulten (Chicago: University of Chicago Press, 2001), pp. 303–72.

18. Lucia Foster, John Haltiwanger, and C. J. Krizan, "Market Selection, Reallocation, and Restructuring in the U.S. Retail Sector in the 1990s," *Review of Economics and Statistics* 88, no. 4 (2006): 748–58.

19. See William J. Baumol, *The Microtheory of Innovative Entrepreneurship* (Princeton, NJ: Princeton University Press, 2010).

20. For a useful overview of the relevant literature, see Fabio Schiantarelli, "Product Market Regulation and Macroeconomic Performance: A Review of the Cross-Country Evidence," Boston College Working Paper 623, August 4, 1988.

21. See Simeon Djankov, Caralee McLiesh, and Rita Ramalho, "Regulation and Growth," *Economics Letters* 92, no. 3 (2006): 295–401; Norman V. Loayza, Ana María Oviedo, and Luis Servén, "Regulation and Macroeconomic Performance," World Bank Policy Research Working Paper no. 3469, September 2004; and Kees Koedijk and Jeroen Kremers, "Market Opening, Regulation and Growth in Europe," *Economic Policy* 11, no. 23 (1996): 443–67.

22. See Giuseppe Nicoletti and Stefano Scarpetta, "Regulation, Productivity, and Growth," World Bank Policy Research Working Paper no. 2944, January 2003; Koedijk and Kremers, "Market Opening, Regulation, and Growth in Europe." For findings that product market regulation reduces the level of TFP (as opposed to the TFP growth rate), see Romain Bouis, Romain Duval, and Fabrice Murtin, "The Policy and Institutional Drivers of Economic Growth across OECD and Non-OECD Economies," Organisation for Economic Co-operation and Development, Economics Department Working Paper no. 843, February 14, 2011; Stefano Scarpetta, Philip Hemmings, Thierry Tressel, and Jaejoon Woo, "The Role of Policy and Institutions for Productivity and Firm Dynamics: Evidence from Micro and Industry Data," Organisation for Economic Co-operation and Development, Economics Department Working Paper no. 329, April 23, 2002. For a finding that reductions in product

market regulation lead to higher labor productivity growth, see Michele Cincera and Olivia Galgau, "Impact of Market Entry and Exit on EU Productivity and Growth Performance," *European Economy*, European Commission, Directorate-General for Economic and Financial Affairs, Economic Paper no. 222, February 2005.

23. See Andrea Bassanini and Ekkehard Ernst, "Labour Market Institutions, Product Market Regulation, and Innovation," Organisation for Economic Co-operation and Development, Economics Department Working Paper no. 316, January 16, 2002.

24. See Rachel Griffith and Rupert Harrison, "The Link between Product Market Reform and Macro-economic Performance," European Commission, Directorate-General for Economic and Financial Affairs, Economic Paper no. 209, August 2004; Alberto Alesina, Silvia Ardagna, Giuseppe Nicoletti, and Fabio Schiantarelli, "Regulation and Investment," National Bureau of Economic Research Working Paper no. 9560, March 2003.

25. See Griffith and Harrison, "The Link between Product Market Reform and Macro-economic Performance"; Giuseppe Nicoletti, Andrea Bassanini, Ekkhard Ernst, Sébastien Jean, Paul Santiago, and Paul Swaim, "Product and Labour Markets Interactions in OECD Countries," Organisation for Economic Co-operation and Development, Economics Department Working Paper no. 312, December 14, 2001.

26. Judith Chevalier and Fiona Scott Morton, "State Casket Sales Restrictions: A Useless Undertaking?" *Journal of Law and Economics* 51, no. 1 (February 2008): 1–23; Francine LaFontaine and Fiona Scott Morton, "State Franchise Laws, Dealer Terminations, and the Auto Crisis," *Journal of Economic Perspectives* 24, no. 3 (Summer 2010): 233–50.

27. See Michael Mandel and Diana G. Carew, "Regulatory Improvement Commission: A Politically Viable Approach to U.S. Regulatory Reform," Progressive Policy Institute Policy Memo, May 2013, http://www.progressivepolicy.org/wp-content/uploads/2013/05/05.2013-Mandel-Carew_Regulatory-Improvement-Commission_A-Politically-Viable-Approach-to-US-Regulatory-Reform.pdf.

Chapter 3

1. See Carmen M. Reinhart and Kenneth S. Rogoff, *This Time It's Different: Eight Centuries of Financial Folly* (Princeton, NJ: Princeton University Press, 2011).

2. See Tyler Atkinson, David Luttrell, and Harvey Rosenblum, "How Bad Was It? The Costs and Consequences of the 2007–09 Financial Crisis," Federal Reserve Bank of Dallas Staff Paper no. 20, July 2013, https://dallasfed.org/assets/documents/research/staff/staff1301.pdf.

3. See Jon Bakija, Adam Cole, and Bradley T. Heim, "Jobs and Income Growth of Top Earners and the Causes of Changing Income Inequality," unpublished working paper, April 2012, https://web.williams.edu/Economics/wp/BakijaColeHeim JobsIncomeGrowthTopEarners.pdf.

4. See Tyler Cowen, "The Inequality That Matters," *American Interest* 6, no. 3 (January 1, 2011), http://www.the-american-interest.com/2011/01/01/the-inequality-that-matters/.

5. http://equitablegrowth.org/equitablog/must-read-steve-teles-the-scourge-of-upward-redistribution-2/.

6. William Lazonick, "Profits without Prosperity," *Harvard Business Review* (September 2014), https://hbr.org/2014/09/profits-without-prosperity.

7. See Robin Greenwood and David Scharfstein, "The Growth of Finance," *Journal of Economic Perspectives* 27, no. 2 (Spring 2013): 3–28.

8. Justin Lahart, "Number of the Week: Finance's Share of Economy Continues to Grow," *Wall Street Journal*, December 10, 2011, http://blogs.wsj.com/economics/2011/12/10/number-of-the-week-finances-share-of-economy-continues-to-grow/.

9. General Accounting Office, "Financial Audit: Resolution Trust Corporation's 1995 and 1994 Financial Statements," July 1996, http://www.gao.gov/archive/1996/ai96123.pdf.

10. See David Min, "For the Last Time, Fannie and Freddie Didn't Cause the Housing Crisis," *The Atlantic*, December 16, 2011, http://www.theatlantic.com/business/archive/2011/12/for-the-last-time-fannie-and-freddie-didnt-cause-the-housing-crisis/250121/.

11. Charles W. Calomiris and Stephen H. Haber, *Fragile by Design: The Political Origins of Banking Crises and Scarce Credit* (Princeton, NJ: Princeton University Press, 2014), p. 207.

12. Calomiris and Haber, *Fragile by Design*, p. 253.

13. See Min, "For the Last Time, Fannie and Freddie Didn't Cause the Housing Crisis."

14. See Neil Bhutta, "GSE Activity and Mortgage Supply in Lower-Income and Minority Neighborhoods: The Effect of the Affordable Housing Goals," *Journal of Real Estate Finance and Economics* 45, no. 1 (2012): 238–61.

15. "Comradely Capitalism," *The Economist*, August 20, 2016, http://www.economist.com/news/briefing/21705316-how-america-accidentally-nationalised-its-mortgage-market-comradely-capitalism.

16. Vernon Smith, Gary L. Suchanek, and Arlington Williams, "Bubbles, Crashes, and Endogenous Expectations in Experimental Spot Asset Markets," *Econometrica* 56, no. 5 (1988): 1119–51.

17. Òscar Jordà, Moritz Schularik, and Alan M. Taylor, "Leveraged Bubbles," National Bureau of Economic Research Working Paper no. 21486, August 2015, http://www.nber.org/papers/w21486.pdf.

18. Quoted in Anat Admati and Martin Hellwig, *The Bankers' New Clothes: What's Wrong with Banking and What to Do about It* (Princeton, NJ: Princeton University Press, 2013), p. 6.

19. The Modigliani-Miller theorem also assumes no transaction costs and no market inefficiencies like asymmetric information.

20. John H. Cochrane, "Equity-Financed Banking and a Run-Free Financial System," 2016, https://faculty.chicagobooth.edu/john.cochrane/research/papers/run-free_talk_mn_2016.pdf.

21. Gregory Phelan, "Financial Intermediation, Leverage, and Macroeconomic Instability," unpublished working paper, January 20, 2016, http://papers.ssrn.com/sol3/papers.cfm?abstract_id=2838423.

22. See Mark Carlson and David C. Wheelock, "Did the Founding of the Federal Reserve Affect the Vulnerability of the Interbank System to Contagion Risk?", Bank of International Settlements Working Paper no. 598, December 2016, http://www.bis.org/publ/work598.pdf; Andrew G. Haldane, "Banking on the State," September 25, 2009, http://www.bis.org/review/r091111e.pdf.

23. Cowen, "The Inequality That Matters."
24. Eric A. Posner, "How Do Bank Regulators Determine Capital Adequacy Requirements?", Coase-Sandor Institute for Law and Economics Working Paper no. 698 (2nd series), September 2014, http://chicagounbound.uchicago.edu/cgi/viewcontent.cgi?article=2370&context=law_and_economics.
25. For a good discussion of what Dodd-Frank did and didn't accomplish on capital regulation, see Mark Calabria, "Did Dodd-Frank Increase Bank Capital?", Alt-M (blog), March 18, 2016, http://www.alt-m.org/2016/03/18/did-dodd-frank-increase-bank-capital/.
26. Admati and Hellwig, The Bankers' New Clothes, pp. 176–91.
27. Charles W. Calomiris, "What's Wrong with Prudential Bank Regulation and How to Fix It," testimony before the U.S. House Committee on Financial Services, July 23, 2015, http://financialservices.house.gov/uploadedfiles/hhrg-114-ba00-wstate-ccalomiris-20150723.pdf.
28. John H. Cochrane, "Toward a Run-Free Financial System," April 16, 2014, http://papers.ssrn.com/sol3/papers.cfm?abstract_id=2425883.
29. Merton H. Miller, "Do the M&M Propositions Apply to Banks?", Journal of Banking & Finance 19 (1995): 483–89.
30. See Calomiris and Haber, p. 7.
31. See, e.g., Ross Levine, "Financial Development and Economic Growth: Views and Agenda," Journal of Economic Literature 35 (June 1997): 688–726.
32. Stephen G. Cecchetti and Enisse Kharroubi, "Reassessing the Impact of Finance on Growth," Bank of International Settlements Working Paper no. 381, July 2012; Stephen G. Cecchetti and Enisse Kharroubi, "Why Does Financial Sector Growth Crowd Out Real Economic Growth?", BIS Working Paper no. 490, February 2015; Jean-Louis Arcand, Enrico Berkes, and Ugo Panizza, "Too Much Finance?", International Monetary Fund Working Paper 12/161, June 2012, https://www.imf.org/external/pubs/ft/wp/2012/wp12161.pdf.
33. Cecchetti and Kharroubi, "Reassessing the Impact of Finance on Growth."
34. William Easterly, Roumeen Islam, and Joseph E. Stiglitz, "Shaken and Stirred: Explaining Growth Volatility," Annual World Bank

Conference on Development Economics, January 2000, http://siteresources.worldbank.org/DEC/Resources/28040_shaken_and_stirred.pdf.

35. Gary Ramey and Valerie A. Ramey, "Cross-Country Evidence on the Link between Volatility and Growth," *American Economic Review* 85, no. 5 (December 1995): 1138–51, http://econweb.ucsd.edu/~vramey/research/Ramey_Ramey_Volatility.pdf.

36. See, e.g., Thorsten Beck, Berrak Büyükkarabacak, Felix K. Rioja, Neven T. Valev, "Who Gets the Credit? And Does It Matter? Household vs. Firm Lending across Countries," *B.E. Journal of Macroeconomics* 12, no. 1 (2012), http://www2.gsu.edu/~ecofkr/papers/published_version_BEJM.pdf.

37. See Tullio Jappelli and Marco Pagano, "Savings, Growth, and Liquidity Constraints," *Quarterly Journal of Economics* 109, no. 1, (1994): 83–109.

38. See Cecchetti and Kharroubi, "Why Does Financial Sector Growth Crowd Out Real Economic Growth?"

39. See Greenwood and Scharfstein, "The Growth of Finance," p. 5.

40. Thomas Phillippon and Ariell Reshef, "Wages and Human Capital in the U.S. Financial Industry: 1909–2006," *Quarterly Journal of Economics* 127, no. 4 (November 2012): 1551–609, http://pages.stern.nyu.edu/~tphilipp/papers/pr_qje2012.pdf.

41. Amy Binder, "Career Funnelling: How Elite Students Learn to Define and Desire 'Prestigious' Jobs," *Sociology of Education* 89, no. 1 (2016): 20–39.

42. See Admati and Hellwig, *The Bankers' New Clothes*, pp. 122–27.

Chapter 4

1. "U.S. Patent Activity: Calendar Years 1790 to the Present," U.S. Patent and Trademark Office, http://www.uspto.gov/web/offices/ac/ido/oeip/taf/h_counts.htm.

2. See Luis Aguiar, Néstor Duch-Brown, and Joel Waldfogel, "Revenue, New Products, and the Evolution of Music Quality since Napster," Institute for Prospective Technological Studies Digital Economy Working Paper 2015/03, 2015, p. 3, https://ec.europa.eu/jrc/sites/default/files/JRC90047_Vintage_quality.pdf.

3. Glynn S. Lunney Jr., "Copyright on the Internet: Consumer Copying and Collectives," in *The Evolution and Equilibrium of Copyright in the Digital Age*, ed. Susy Frankel and Daniel Gervais (Cambridge: Cambridge University Press, 2014), pp. 292–93.

4. Motion Picture Association of America, Theatrical Market Statistics 2014, p. 21, http://www.mpaa.org/wp-content/uploads/2015/03/MPAA-Theatrical-Market-Statistics-2014.pdf.

5. "Traditional Print Book Production Dipped Slightly in 2013," August 5, 2014, http://www.bowker.com/news/2014/Traditional-Print-Book-Production-Dipped-Slightly-in-2013.html; "Self-Publishing Continues to Grow in U.S., Says Bowker," October 28, 2014, http://www.bowker.com/news/2014/Self-Publishing-Continues-to-Grow-in-US-Says--Bowker.html.

6. Josh Lerner, "Patent Protection and Innovation over 150 Years," National Bureau of Economic Research Working Paper no. 8977, June 2002, p. 2, http://www.nber.org/papers/w8977.pdf.

7. Adam B. Jaffe, "The U.S. Patent System in Transition: Policy Innovation and the Innovation Process," *Research Policy* 29 (2000): pp. 531–77.

8. Petra Moser, "How Do Patent Laws Influence Innovation? Evidence from Nineteenth-Century World Fairs," National Bureau of Economic Research Working Paper no. 9909, August 2003, p. 1. She did find that patent laws affected the focus of innovative activity. Specifically, in countries without patent laws, innovations were concentrated in areas where secrecy was easier to maintain.

9. See Alex Tabarrok, *Launching the Innovation Renaissance: A New Path to Bring Smart Ideas to Market Fast* (New York: TED Books, 2011).

10. Fritz Machlup, "An Economic Review of the Patent System," Study of the Subcommittee on Patents, Trademarks, and Copyrights of the Committee on the Judiciary," U.S. Senate, 85th Congress, 2nd session, 1958.

11. Joan Robinson, *The Accumulation of Capital* (London: Macmillan, 1956), p. 87.

12. See Carl Shapiro, "Navigating the Patent Thicket: Cross Licenses, Patent Pools, and Standard Setting," in *Innovation Policy and the*

Economy, vol. 1, ed. Adam B. Jaffe, Josh Lerner, and Scott Stern (Cambridge, MA: MIT Press, 2001), pp. 119–50.

13. For a discussion of the tragedy of the anticommons in the intellectual property context and elsewhere, see Michael Heller, *The Gridlock Economy: How Too Much Ownership Wrecks Markets, Stops Innovation, and Costs Lives* (New York: Basic Books, 2008).

14. David Kravets, "Web Browsing Is Copyright Infringement, Publishers Argue," *Ars Technica*, June 5, 2014, http://arstechnica.com/tech-policy/2014/06/web-browsing-is-copyright-infringement-publishers-argue/.

15. Fred von Lohmann, "Google Cache Ruled Legal," Electronic Frontier Foundation, January 25, 2006, https://www.eff.org/deeplinks/2006/01/google-cache-ruled-fair-use.

16. For a thought experiment on how one hypothetical law professor's typical day could include 83 acts of copyright infringement with potential liability of $12.45 million (in addition to possible imprisonment), see John Tehranian, "Infringement Nation," *Utah Law Review* (2007): 537.

17. For percentages of books in the public domain and under copyright but out of print, see Jeffrey Toobin, "Google's Moon Shot," *New Yorker*, February 5, 2007, http://www.newyorker.com/magazine/2007/02/05/googles-moon-shot.

18. See Timothy B. Lee, "Save the Orphan (Works)," Cato Institute TechKnowledge no. 117, June 30, 2008.

19. Peter Baldwin, *The Copyright Wars: Three Centuries of Trans-Atlantic Battle* (Princeton, NJ: Princeton University Press, 2014), p. 366.

20. See Kevin Waddell, "The Research Pirates of the Dark Web," *Atlantic*, February 9, 2016, http://www.theatlantic.com/technology/archive/2016/02/the-research-pirates-of-the-dark-web/461829/; Nikhil Sonnad, "The Website That Offered 47 Million Pirated Academic Papers Is Back," *Quartz*, February 14, 2016, http://qz.com/616677/the-website-that-offered-47-million-pirated-academic-papers-is-back/.

21. See Edward Felten, "The Chilling Effects of the DMCA," *Slate*, March 29, 2013, http://www.slate.com/articles/technology/future_tense/2013/03/dmca_chilling_effects_how_copyright_law_hurts_security_research.html.

22. See James Bessen and Michael J. Meurer, *Patent Failure: How Judges, Bureaucrats, and Lawyers Put Innovators at Risk* (Princeton, NJ: Princeton University Press, 2008), Figure 6.5, p. 139.

23. Timothy B. Lee and Christina Mulligan, "Scaling the Patent System," *NYU Annual Survey of American Law* 68, no. 289 (2012), http://digitalcommons.law.uga.edu/cgi/viewcontent.cgi?article=1911&context=fac_artchop/913.

24. Executive Office of the President, "Patent Assertion and U.S. Innovation," Council of Economic Advisers, National Economic Council and Office of Science and Technology Policy, June 2013, http://www.whitehouse.gov/sites/default/files/docs/patent_report.pdf.

25. James Bessen and Michael Meurer, "The Direct Costs from NPE Disputes," Boston University School of Law Working Paper 12-34, June 25, 2012, https://www.bu.edu/law/faculty/scholarship/workingpapers/documents/BessenJ_MeurerM062512rev062812.pdf.

26. See Amy Kapczynksi, "Four Hypotheses on Intellectual Property and Inequality," Working Paper Prepared for the SELA conference, June 11–14, 2015, https://www.law.yale.edu/system/files/documents/pdf/SELA15_Kapczynski_CV_Eng.pdf.

27. Glenn Peeples, "Adele's '25' Is 42 Percent of Total Music Sales This Week," *Billboard.com*, November 24, 2015, http://www.billboard.com/articles/business/6776984/adele-25-42-percent-record-sales-7-5-million-200.

28. Patricia M. Danzon, Andrew Epstein, and Sean Nicholson, "Mergers and Acquisitions in the Pharmaceutical and Biotechnology Industries," National Bureau of Economic Research Working Paper no. 10536, June 2004.

29. Michele Boldrin and David K. Levine, *Against Intellectual Monopoly* (New York: Cambridge University Press, 2008).

30. Google's Ngram viewer shows an exponential takeoff in the term's usage after 1980. See https://books.google.com/ngrams/graph?content=intellectual+property&year_start=1800&year_end=2000&corpus=15&smoothing=3&share=&direct_url=t1%3B%2Cintellectual%20property%3B%2Cc0.

31. See, e.g., Boldrin and Levine, *Against Intellectual Monopoly*.

32. By contrast, in continental Europe there is a strong tradition of viewing copyright as a natural right, but there the justification

tends to focus more on an artistic work's intimate connection to the personality of its author than on the artistic work as a species of property. For the differences generally between American and European approaches to copyright, see Baldwin, *The Copyright Wars: Three Centuries of Trans-Atlantic Battle*.

33. We reject the argument that derivative works are not truly original because they incorporate material from prior works. All creative expression occurs in a cultural context, a cultural commons from which artists draw and to which they make their own original contributions. Goethe's *Faust* is a masterwork of creative genius notwithstanding the fact that he didn't invent the title character. See also *Snow White and the Seven Dwarfs, Pinocchio*, and many other Disney films based on sources in the public domain. As T. S. Eliot once wrote, "Immature poets imitate; mature poets steal."

34. For the seminal article on this topic, see William F. Ogburn and Dorothy Thomas, "Are Inventions Inevitable? A Note on Social Evolution," *Political Science Quarterly* 37, no. 1 (1922): 83–98. For further interesting discussion, see Kevin Kelly, *What Technology Wants* (New York: Viking Adult, 2010), ch. 7.

35. See Christopher A. Cotropia and Mark A. Lemley, "Copying in Patent Law," *North Carolina Law Review* 87, no. 5 (2009): 1421–66.

Chapter 5

1. Morris M. Kleiner, "Occupational Licensing: Protecting the Public Interest or Protectionism?" W. E. Upjohn Institute for Employment Research Policy Paper no. 2011-009, July 2011, http://research.upjohn.org/up_policypapers/9/.

2. Department of the Treasury Office of Economic Policy, Council of Economic Advisers, and Department of Labor, "Occupational Licensing: A Framework for Policymakers," July 2015, pp. 19–20, https://www.whitehouse.gov/sites/default/files/docs/licensing_report_final_nonembargo.pdf.

3. Department of the Treasury Office of Economic Policy, Council of Economic Advisers, and Department of Labor, "Occupational Licensing: A Framework for Policymakers," p. 7.

4. See Dick M. Carpenter II, Lisa Knepper, Angela C. Erickson, and John K. Ross, "License to Work: A National Study of Burdens from Occupational Licensing," Institute for Justice, May 2012, https://www.ij.org/licensetowork.

5. See Carl Shapiro, "Investment, Moral Hazard, and Occupational Licensing," *Review of Economic Studies* 53, no. 5 (1986): 843–62, http://www.jstor.org/stable/2297722.

6. See Adam B. Summers, "Occupational Licensing: Ranking the States and Exploring Alternatives," Reason Foundation Policy Study no. 361, July 2007, http://reason.org/news/show/occupational-licensing-ranking.

7. See Carpenter et al., "License to Work."

8. See Carpenter et al., "License to Work."

9. See Morris M. Kleiner and Robert T. Kudrle, "Does Regulation Affect Economic Outcomes? The Case of Dentistry," *Journal of Law and Economics* 43, no. 2 (2000): 547–82. But for different results, see Arlene Holen, *The Economics of Dental Licensing*, US Department of Health and Human Services, 1978.

10. See Morris M. Kleiner, *Stages of Occupational Regulation: Analysis of Case Studies* (Kalamazoo, MI: W. E. Upjohn Institute for Employment Research, 2013). For different findings regarding mortgage brokerage, see Lan Shi and Yan Zhang, "The Effect of Mortgage Broker Licensing on Loan Origination Standards and Defaults under the Originate-to-Distribute Model: Evidence from the U.S. Mortgage Market," February 2013, http://papers.ssrn.com/sol3/paperscfm?abstract_id=2220013.

11. Joshua D. Angrist and Jonathan Guryan, "Teacher Testing, Teacher Education, and Teacher Characteristics," *American Economic Review* 94, no. 2 (2004): 241–46.

12. Dick M. Carpenter II, "Blooming Nonsense: Do Claims about the Consumer Benefit of Licensure Withstand Empirical Scrutiny?" *Regulation* (Spring 2011): 44–47, http://object.cato.org/sites/cato.org/files/serials/files/regulation/2011/4/regv34n1-8.pdf.

13. David Skarbek, "Occupational Licensing and Asymmetric Information: Post-Hurricane Evidence from Florida," *Cato Journal* 28, no. 1 (2008): 73–82, http://object.cato.org/sites/cato.org/files/serials/files/cato-journal/2008/1/cj28n1-5.pdf.

14. Morris M. Kleiner and Alan B. Krueger, "Analyzing the Extent and Influence of Occupational Licensing," *Journal of Labor Economics* 31, no. 2, pt. 2 (2013): S173–202.

15. Morris M. Kleiner, *Licensing Occupations: Ensuring Quality or Restricting Competition?* (Kalamazoo, MI: W. E. Upjohn Institute for Employment Research, 2006).

16. Morris M. Kleiner, "Reforming Occupational Licensing Policies," Brookings Institution, Hamilton Project Discussion Paper 2015-01, January 2015, http://www.brookings.edu/~/media/research/files/papers/2015/01/28%20reforming%20occupational%20licensing%20kleiner/reform_occupational_licensing_policies_kleiner_v4.pdf.

17. Kleiner, *Licensing Occupations*, p. 115.

18. Andrew Bender, "Uber's Astounding Rise: Overtaking Taxis in Key Markets," *Forbes*, April 10, 2015, http://www.forbes.com/sites/andrewbender/2015/04/10/ubers-astounding-rise-overtaking-taxis-in-key-markets/#4d6699a922ef.

19. Peter Cohen, Robert Hahn, Jonathan Hall, Steven Levitt, and Robert Metcalfe, "Using Big Data to Estimate Consumer Surplus: The Case of Uber," National Bureau of Economic Research Working Paper No. 22627, September 2016, http://www.nber.org/papers/w22627.

20. Scott Wallstein, "Has Uber Forced Taxi Drivers to Up Their Game?" *Atlantic*, July 9, 2015, http://www.theatlantic.com/business/archive/2015/07/uber-taxi-drivers-complaints-chicago-newyork/397931/.

21. Kleiner, "Reforming Occupational Licensing Policies."

22. Kleiner and Krueger, "Analyzing the Extent and Influence of Occupational Licensing."

23. Angrist and Guryan, "Teacher Testing, Teacher Education, and Teacher Characteristics."

24. Maya N. Federman, David E. Harrington, and Kathy J. Krynski, "The Impact of State Licensing Regulations on Low-Skilled Immigrants: The Case of Vietnamese Manicurists," *American Economic Review* 96, no. 2 (2006): 237–41.

25. Beth Avery, "A Mistake That Lasts a Lifetime," *Democracy*, October 7, 2016, http://democracyjournal.org/arguments/a-mistake-that-lasts-a-lifetime/.

26. Department of Labor et al., "Occupational Licensing: A Framework for Policymakers," pp. 35–37.
27. Janna E. Johnson and Morris M. Kleiner, "Is Occupational Licensing a Barrier to Interstate Migration?" paper presented at Population Association of America 2015 Annual Meeting, San Diego, CA, April 30–May 2, 2015, http://paa2015.princeton.edu/uploads/152473.
28. Morris M. Kleiner, "Occupational Licensing," *Journal of Economic Perspectives* 14, no. 1 (2000): 196, https://www.aeaweb.org/articles?id=10.1257/jep.14.4.189.
29. http://www.nytimes.com/packages/html/newsgraphics/2012/0115-one-percent-occupations/.
30. See Shirley V. Svorny, "Beyond Medical Licensure," *Regulation*, Spring 2015, pp. 26–29.
31. See Shirley Svorny, "Medical Licensing: An Obstacle to Affordable, Quality Care," Cato Institute Policy Analysis no. 621, September 17, 2008, p. 7.
32. See Svorny, "Medical Licensing"; Shirley Svorny, "Could Mandatory Caps on Medical Malpractice Damages Harm Consumers?" Cato Institute Policy Analysis no. 685, October 20, 2011; Katherine Baicker and Amitabh Chandra, "Defensive Medicine and Disappearing Doctors?" *Regulation*, Fall 2005, pp. 24–31.
33. Adriana D. Kugler and Robert M. Sauer, "Doctors without Borders? Relicensing Requirements and Negative Selection in the Market for Physicians," *Journal of Labor Economics* 23, no. 3 (July 2005): 437–66.
34. Miriam J. Laugeson and Sherry A. Glied, "Higher Fees Paid to US Physicians Drive Higher Spending for Physician Services Compared to Other Countries," *Health Affairs* 30, no. 9 (2011); 1647–56, http://content.healthaffairs.org/content/30/9/1647.full.html.
35. See Chris Conover, "Are U.S. Doctors Paid Too Much?" *Forbes*, May 28, 2013, http://www.forbes.com/sites/theapothecary/2013/05/28/are-u-s-doctors-paid-too-much/#1159a24a3e5c; Jeremy White, Robert Gebelhoff, Ford Fessenden, and Shan Carter, "The Top 1 Percent: What Jobs Do They Have?" *New York Times*, January 15, 2012, http://www.nytimes.com/packages/html/newsgraphics/2012/0115-one-percent-occupations/.

36. "Medical School Applicants, Enrollees Reach New Highs," Association of American Medical Colleges news release, October 22, 2015, https://www.aamc.org/newsroom/newsreleases/446400/applicant-and-enrollment-data.html.

37. http://www.nrmp.org/wp-content/uploads/2016/04/Main-Match-Results-and-Data-2016.pdf.

38. Melissa Bailey, "After Earning an MD, She's Headed Back to School—To Become a Nurse," STAT, November 28, 2016, https://www.statnews.com/2016/11/28/residency-failed-to-match/?s_campaign=tw&utm_content=buffer4b4a8&utm_medium=social&utm_source=twitter.com&utm_campaign=buffer.

39. Morris M. Kleiner, Allison Marier, Kyoung Won Park, and Coady Wing, "Relaxing Occupational Licensing Requirements: Analyzing Wages and Prices for a Medical Service," National Bureau of Economic Research Working Paper no. 19906, February 2014.

40. See Dean Baker, "The Compensation of Highly Paid Professionals: How Much Is Rent?" Center for Economic and Policy Research working paper, August 2016, http://cepr.net/images/stories/reports/highly-paid-professionals-2016-08.pdf.

41. White et al., "The Top 1 Percent: What Jobs Do They Have?"

42. Morris M. Kleiner and Kyoung Won Park, "Battles among Licensed Occupations: Analyzing Government Regulations on Labor Market Outcomes for Dentists and Hygienists," National Bureau of Economic Research Working Paper no. 16560, November 2010.

43. See Mario Pagliero, "The Impact of Potential Labor Supply on Licensing Exam Difficulty," *Labour Economics* 25 (2013): 141–52.

44. See, e.g., Robert Ambrogi, "Latest Legal Victory Has LegalZoom Poised for Growth," *ABA Journal*, August 1, 2014, http://www.abajournal.com/magazine/article/latest_legal_victory_has_legalzoom_poised_for_growth.

45. Philip K. Howard has been an eloquent chronicler of the perils of excessive legalism. See, most recently, his *The Rule of Nobody: Saving America from Dead Laws and Broken Government* (New York: W. W. Norton, 2014).

46. Clifford Winston, Robert W. Crandall, and Vikram Maheshri, *First Thing We Do, Let's Deregulate All the Lawyers* (Washington, DC: Brookings Institution Press, 2011), Table 3.1.
47. Winston et al., *First Thing We Do, Let's Deregulate All the Lawyers*.

Chapter 6

1. See William A. Fischel, "An Economic History of Zoning and a Cure for Its Exclusionary Effects," *Urban Studies* 41, no. 2 (2004): 317–40, http://www.dartmouth.edu/~wfischel/Papers/02-03.pdf.
2. See Edward L. Glaeser, Joseph Gyourko, and Raven E. Saks, "Why Have Housing Prices Gone Up?" National Bureau of Economic Research Working Paper no. 11129, February 2005, http://www.nber.org/papers/w11129.pdf.
3. Glaeser et al., "Why Have Housing Prices Gone Up?"
4. Glaeser et al., "Why Have Housing Prices Gone Up?"
5. See Edward L. Glaeser and Bryce A. Ward, "The Causes and Consequences of Land Use Regulation: Evidence from Greater Boston," *Journal of Urban Economics* 65 (2009): 265–78, http://scholar.harvard.edu/files/glaeser/files/the_causes_and_consequences_of_land_use_regulation_evidence_from_greater_boston_2009.pdf.
6. See Edward L. Glaeser and Joseph Gyourko, "The Impact of Building Restrictions on Housing Affordability," *Federal Reserve Bank of New York Economic Policy Review* 9, no. 2 (2003): 21–39, http://www.newyorkfed.org/research/epr/03v09n2/0306glae.pdf.
7. See Edward L. Glaeser, Joseph Gyourko, and Raven Saks, "Why Is Manhattan So Expensive? Regulation and the Rise of Housing Prices," *Journal of Law and Economics* 48, no. 2 (2005): 331–69, http://repository.upenn.edu/cgi?article+1007&context=penniur_papers.
8. See Jaison R. Abel, Ishita Dey, and Todd M. Gabe, "Productivity and the Density of Human Capital," Federal Reserve Bank of New York Staff Report no. 440, March 2010 (revised September 2011), http://www.newyorkfed.org/research/staff_reports/sr440.pdf.
9. See Enrico Moretti, *The New Geography of Jobs* (New York: Houghton Mifflin, 2012), p. 96.

10. See Robert J. Barro and Xavier Sala-i-Martin, "Convergence across States and Regions," *Brookings Papers on Economic Activity* 22, no. 1 (1991): 107–82.

11. Peter Ganong and Daniel Shoag, "Why Has Regional Income Convergence in the U.S. Declined?" Harvard Kennedy School Faculty Research Working Paper RWP12-028, updated draft January 2015, https://scholar.harvard.edu/files/shoag/files/why_has_regional_income_convergence_in_the_us_declined_01.pdf.

12. Ganong and Shoag, "Why Has Regional Income Convergence in the U.S. Declined?"

13. See Moretti, *The New Geography of Jobs*, p. 77.

14. See Moretti, *The New Geography of Jobs*, pp. 95–97.

15. See Antonio Ciccone and Robert E. Hall, "Productivity and the Density of Economic Activity," *American Economic Review* 86, no. 1 (1996): 54–70, http://web.stanford.edu/~rehall/Productivity-AER-March-1996.pdf; Morris A. Davis, Jonas D. M. Fisher, and Toni M. Whited, "Macroeconomic Implications of Agglomeration," *Econometrica* 82, no. 2 (2014): 731–64; Morikaw Masayuki, "Economics of Density in Service Industries: An Analysis of Personal Service Industries Based on Establishment-Level Data," Research Institute of Economy, Trade and Industry Discussion Paper Series 08-E-023, July 2008; Timothy F. Harris and Yanis M. Ioannides, "Productivity and Metropolitan Density," Discussion Paper Series, Department of Economics, Tufts University, May 15, 2000.

16. See Jaison R. Abel, Ishita Dey, and Todd M. Gabe, "Productivity and the Density of Human Capital," Federal Reserve Bank of New York Staff Report no. 440, March 2010 (revised September 2011), http://www.newyorkfed.org/research/staff_reports/sr440.pdf.

17. See Moretti, *The New Geography of Jobs*, pp. 94–95.

18. Enrico Moretti, "Estimating the Social Return to Higher Education: Evidence from Longitudinal and Repeated Cross-Sectional Data," *Journal of Econometrics* 121 (2004): 175–212.

19. Ryan Avent, *The Gated City* (Amazon Digital Services, Kindle Edition, 2011).

20. See Edward L. Glaeser and Kristina Tobio, "The Rise of the Sunbelt," National Bureau of Economic Research Working

Paper no. 13071, April 2007, http://www.nber.org/papers/w13071.pdf.

21. See Ganong and Shoag, "Why Has Regional Convergence in the U.S. Declined?"

22. Enrico Moretti and Chiang-Tai Hsieh, "Why Do Cities Matter? Local Growth and Aggregate Growth," National Bureau of Economic Research Working Paper no. 21154, May 2015, http://www.nber.org/papers/w21154.

23. See Jesse Bricker et al., "Changes in U.S. Family Finances from 2010 to 2013: Evidence from the Survey of Consumer Finances," *Federal Reserve Bulletin* 100, no. 4 (2014), http://www.federalreserve.gov/pubs/bulletin/2014/pdf/scf14.pdf.

24. See Jonathan Rothwell and Douglas S. Massey, "The Effect of Density Zoning on Racial Segregation in U.S. Urban Areas," *Urban Affairs Review* 44, no. 6 (2009): 779–806, http://www.thecyberhood.net/documents/papers/uar09.pdf; Jonathan Rothwell and Douglas S. Massey, "Density Zoning and Class Segregation in U.S. Metropolitan Areas," *Social Science Quarterly* 91, no. 5 (2010): 1123–43. See also Matthew Resseger, "The Impact of Land Use Regulation on Racial Segregation: Evidence from Massachusetts Zoning Borders," Harvard University, November 26, 2013, http://scholar.harvard.edu/files/resseger/files/resseger_jmp_11_25.pdf.

25. See, for example, David M. Cutler and Edward L. Glaeser, "Are Ghettos Good or Bad?" *Quarterly Journal of Economics* 112, no. 3 (1997): 827–72.

26. See Raven Molloy, Christopher L. Smith, and Abigail Wozniak, "Internal Migration in the United States," *Journal of Economic Perspectives* 25, no. 3 (Summer 2011): 173–96.

27. Scott Winship, "When Moving Matters: Residential and Economic Mobility Trends in America, 1880–2010," Manhattan Institute e21 Report no. 2, November 2015, https://www.manhattan-institute.org/html/when-moving-matters-residential-and-economic-mobility-trends-america-1880-2010-8048.html.

28. Matthew Rognlie, "Deciphering the Fall and Rise of the Net Capital Share," *Brookings Papers on Economic Activity* (Spring 2015): 1–54, https://scholar.harvard.edu/files/shoag/files/why_has_regional_income_convergence_in_the_us_declined_01.pdf.

Chapter 7

1. Mancur Olson, *The Logic of Collective Action* (Cambridge, MA: Harvard University Press, 1965).
2. On the psychological basis of risk aversion, see Daniel Kahneman and Amos Tversky, "Prospect Theory: An Analysis of Decision under Risk," *Econometrica* 47, no. 2 (March 1979): 263–92; on the impact of government policy on the growth of supportive interests, see Beth Leech, Frank Baumgartner, Timothy LaPira, and Nicholas Semanko, "Drawing Lobbyists to Washington: Government Activity and the Demand for Advocacy," *Political Research Quarterly* 58, no. 1 (March 2005): 19–30.
3. Jonathan Rauch, *Government's End* (New York: Public Affairs, 1999).
4. Joseph Bessette, *The Mild Voice of Reason: Deliberative Democracy and American National Government* (Chicago: University of Chicago Press, 1994).
5. Frank Baumgartner, Jeffrey Berry, Marie Hojnacki, David Kimball, and Beth Leech, *Lobbying and Policy Change: Who Wins, Who Loses and Why* (Chicago: University of Chicago Press, 2009).
6. Lee Drutman, "The Solution to Lobbying Is More Lobbying," *Washington Post*, April 29, 2015, https://www.washingtonpost.com/blogs/monkey-cage/wp/2015/04/29/the-solution-to-lobbying-is-more-lobbying/.
7. Mark Smith, *American Business and Political Power: Public Opinion, Elections and Democracy* (Chicago: University of Chicago Press, 2000).
8. Frank Baumgarter and Bryan Jones, *Agendas and Instability in American Politics* (Chicago: University of Chicago Press, 1993); Bryan Jones and Frank Baumgartner, *The Politics of Attention: How Government Prioritizes Problems* (Chicago: University of Chicago Press, 2005).
9. Richard Hall and Frank Wayman find that money buys substantial influence over relatively lower-profile activities of members of Congress in committees, but relatively less in votes on the floor. This is consistent with the hypothesis that money is most influential when the spotlight is dimmest. "Buying Time: Moneyed Interests and the Mobilization of Bias in Congressional

Committees," *American Political Science Review* 84, no. 3 (September 1990): 797–820.

10. Martha Derthick and Paul Quirk, *The Politics of Deregulation* (Washington, DC: Brookings Institution, 1985).

11. Elizabeth Warren, "Unsafe at Any Rate," *Democracy Journal* 5 (Summer 2007).

12. Mark Schmitt, "Machinery of Progress," *American Prospect*, December 8, 2009.

13. Ilya Somin, *The Grasping Hand: Kelo v. The City of New London and the Limits of Eminent Domain* (Chicago: University of Chicago Press, 2015).

14. The general phenomenon of the erosion of public interest legislation is discussed in Eric Patashnik, *Reforms at Risk* (Princeton, NJ: Princeton University Press, 2008).

15. Arthur Wilmarth, "Turning a Blind Eye: Why Washington Keeps Giving In to Wall Street," *University of Cincinnati Law Review* 81, no. 4 (2013): 1283-1446.

16. Richard Hall and Alan Deardorff, "Lobbying as Legislative Subsidy," *American Political Science Review* 100, no. 1 (February 2006): 69–84; Richard Hall and Frank Wayman, "Buying Time: Moneyed Interests and the Mobilization of Bias," *American Political Science Review* 84, no. 3 (September 1990): 797–820.

17. Cass Sunstein, *Simpler: The Future of Government* (New York: Simon and Schuster, 2013), p. 175.

18. Lee Drutman, *The Business of America Is Lobbying* (New York: Oxford University Press, 2015).

19. Douglas Arnold, *The Logic of Congressional Action* (New Haven, CT: Yale University Press, 1992).

20. Baumgartner and Jones, *The Politics of Information* (Chicago: University of Chicago Press, 2015), ch. 4.

21. Baumgartner and Jones, *Agendas and Instability.*

22. Charles Geisst, *Wall Street: A History* (New York: Oxford University Press, 2012).

23. James Kwak, "Cultural Capital and the Financial Crisis," in *Preventing Regulatory Capture: Special Interest Influence and How to Limit It*, ed. Dan Carpenter and David Moss (Cambridge: Cambridge University Press, 2013).

24. Anthony Heyes, "Expert Advice and Regulatory Complexity," *Journal of Regulatory Economics* 24, no. 2 (September 2003): 119–33, http://link.springer.com/article/10.1023%2FA%3A1024714610368.

25. David Brooks, "Is Our Country as Good as Our Athletes Are?" *New York Times*, August 19, 2016.

26. William New, "Confidential USTR Emails Show Close Industry Involvement in TPP Negotiations," *Intellectual Property Watch*, May 6, 2015, http://www.ip-watch.org/2015/06/05/confidential-ustr-emails-show-close-industry-involvement-in-tpp-negotiations/.

27. Charles Lindblom, "The Market as Prison," *Journal of Politics* 44, no. 2 (May 1982): 324–36

28. James Gimpel and Frances Lee, "The Check Is in the Mail: Interdistrict Funding Flows in Congressional Elections," *American Journal of Political Science* 52, no. 2 (April 2008): 373–94.

29. Eleanor Powell, "Legislative Consequences of Fundraising Influence," http://www.eleanorneffpowell.com/uploads/8/3/9/3/8393347/powell__2015__-_legislative_consequences_of_fundraising_influence.pdf.

30. Adam Bonica, "Professional Networks, Early Fundraising, and Electoral Success," Scholars Strategy Network Paper, http://www.scholarsstrategynetwork.org/sites/default/files/bonica_professional_networks_early_fundraising_and_electoral_success.pdf.

31. Edward Glaeser, "Preservation Follies," *City Journal*, Spring 2010, http://www.city-journal.org/html/preservation-follies-13279.html.

32. Tim Lee, "How a Rogue Appeals Court Wrecked the Patent System," *Ars Technica*, September 30, 2012, http://arstechnica.com/tech-policy/2012/09/how-a-rogue-appeals-court-wrecked-the-patent-system/.

33. Steven Teles, "Kludgeocracy in America," *National Affairs* 17 (Fall 2013): 97–114.

34. United States Department of the Treasury, Distribution Tables 2016 005b. Washington, DC: Office of Tax Analysis, https://www.treasury.gov/resource-center/tax-policy/tax-analysis/Documents/Retirement-Savings-2016.pdf. While the fees of

401k asset managers are widely recognized, those associated with
plan administration are not. See John Coumarianos, "Why Your
401(k) Fees Aren't Lower," *Wall Street Journal*, November 6, 2016.
35. Christopher Faricy has shown that there is, in fact, a partisan dimension to reliance on the private welfare state, with
Republicans much more likely to expand it compared to the public
welfare state in periods in which they are in control. Christopher
Faricy, *Welfare for the Wealthy* (Cambridge: Cambridge University
Press, 2015).

Chapter 8

1. Jack Walker, "The Organization and Maintenance of Interest
Groups in America," *American Political Science Review* 84
(September 1983): 797–820.
2. L. Caldwell, "Environment: A New Focus for Public Policy?"
Public Administration Review 22 (1963): 132–39.
3. Steven Teles, *The Rise of the Conservative Legal Movement*
(Princeton, NJ: Princeton University Press, 2008), ch. 2.
4. On the centralization of government, see William Lunch, *The
Nationalization of American Politics* (Berkeley: University of
California Press, 1987). On the ways that the courts were opened
to pro-regulatory interests, see Richard Stewart, "The Reformation
of American Administrative Law," *Harvard Law Review* 88, no. 8
(1975): 1667–813.
5. Chris Bosso, *Environment, Inc.* (Lawrence: University Press of
Kansas, 2005).
6. Terry Moe, *Special Interest: Teachers Unions and America's Public
Schools* (Washington, DC: Brookings Institution, 2011).
7. An excellent study of the role of foundations in K–12 education is
Sarah Reckhow, *Follow the Money* (New York: Oxford University
Press, 2012).
8. Jeff Henig, *The End of Exceptionalism in American Education*
(Cambridge, MA: Harvard Education Press, 2013).
9. Reckhow, *Follow the Money*.
10. 246 Cal.App.4th 619 (2016). For a critical analysis of the role of
foundations in Vergara, see Mark Palko, "*Vergara vs. California:
Are the Top 1% Buying Their Version of Education Reform?*"

Washington Post, June 23, 2014, https://www.washingtonpost. com/news/monkey-cage/wp/2014/06/23/vergara-vs-california-are-the-top-0-1-buying-their-version-of-education-reform/.

11. Andrew Kelly, "Turning Lightning into Electricity: Organizing Parents for Education Reform," https://www.aei.org/wp-content/uploads/2014/12/Kelly_Turning-Lightning-Into-Electricity.pdf.

12. Diane Ravitch, *Reign of Error: The Hoax of the Privatization Movement and the Danger to America's Public Schools* (New York: Vintage, 2014).

13. Sarah Reckhow and Jeffrey Snyder, for instance, put the scale of foundation support for political advocacy in education at over $100 million in 2010, and it is certainly more now. Sarah Reckhow and Jeffrey Snyder, "The Expanding Role of Philanthropy in Education Politics," *Education Researcher* 43, no. 4 (2014): 186–95.

14. Erica Goode and Claire Cain Miller, "Backlash by the Bay: Tech Riches Alter a City," *New York Times,* November 24, 2013. The Open Philanthropy Project, the philanthropic arm of Dustin Moskowitz, has already made investments in organizations fighting land-use restrictions, which are described here: http://www. openphilanthropy.org/focus/us-policy/land-use-reform.

15. This section is drawn from Lee Drutman and Steven Teles, "A New Agenda for Political Reform," *Washington Monthly,* March/ April/ May 2015, http://washingtonmonthly.com/magazine/maraprmay-2015/a-new-agenda-for-political-reform/. We are indebted to Lee for allowing us to use it.

16. See Daniel Schuman, "Keeping Congress Competent: Staff Pay, Turnover, and What It Means for Democracy," Sunlight Foundation, December 21, 2010, https://sunlightfoundation. com/blog/2010/12/21/keeping-congress-competent-staff-pay-turnover-and-what-it-means-for-democracy/.

17. Lee Drutman, *The Business of America Is Lobbying* (New York: Oxford University Press, 2015).

18. Nolan McCarty, "Complexity, Capacity, and Capture," in Daniel Carpenter, Steven Croley and David Moss, *Preventing Capture* (Cambridge: Cambridge University Press, 2013).

19. Edward Glaeser and Cass Sunstein, "Regulatory Review for the States," *National Affairs* 20 (Summer 2014).

20. See, e.g., Stuart Shapiro, "Politics and Regulatory Policy Analysis," *Regulation*, Summer 2006, http://object.cato.org/sites/cato.org/files/serials/files/regulation/2006/7/v29n1-7.pdf.

21. *North Carolina Board of Dental Examiners v. FTC*, No. 15-534, 574 U.S. ___ (2015).

22. James Cooper and William Kovacic, "US Convergence with International Competition Norms: Antitrust Law and Public Restraints on Competition," *BU Law Review*, 2010, http://www.internationalcompetitionnetwork.org/uploads/advocacy/adv%20postings/cooper%20&%20kovacic%20(final).pdf.

23. Ross Levine, "The Sentinel: Improving the Governance of Financial Regulation," in *The International Financial Crisis: Have the Rules of Finance Changed?* ed. Asli Demirguc-Kunt, Douglas D. Evanoff and George G. Kaufman (Hackensack, NJ: World Scientific, 2010).

24. The possibilities and limits of distributive analysis are discussed in Lisa Robinson, James Hammitt, and Richard Zeckhauser, "Attention to Distribution in US Regulatory Analyses," *Review of Environmental Economics and Policy* 10, no. 2 (Summer 2016): 308–28.

25. Henig, *The End of Exceptionalism*.

26. David Schleicher, "City Unplanning," *Yale Law Journal* 122, no. 7 (2013): 1670–737; Roderick Hills and David Schleicher, "Planning an Affordable City," *Iowa Law Journal* 101 (2015): 91–136.

27. See Edward Glaeser, *Triumph of the City: How Our Greatest Invention Makes Us Happier, Smarter, Greener, Healthier, and Happier* (New York: Penguin Press, 2011), p. 162.

28. See Edward Glaeser, "Land-Use Restrictions and Other Barriers to Growth," in *Reviving Economic Growth: Policy Proposals from 51 Leading Experts*, ed. Brink Lindsey (Washington, DC: Cato Institute, 2015), p. 95.

29. Diane Wood, "Keynote Address: Is It Time to Abolish the Federal Circuit's Exclusive Jurisdiction in Patent Cases?" *Chicago-Kent Journal of Intellectual Property* 13, no. 1 (Fall 2013): 1–10.

30. William Howell and Terry Moe, *Relic* (New York: Basic Books, 2016).

31. See Teles, *Rise of the Conservative Legal Movement*, ch. 4 and ch. 6.

32. *North Carolina Board of Dental Examiners v. FTC,* No. 15-534, 574 U.S. ___ (2015).
33. *St. Joseph Abbey v. Castille,* 712 F.3d 215 (5th Cir. 2013).
34. *Powers v. Harris,* 379 F.3d 1208 (10th Cir. 2004).
35. *Patel v. Texas Department of Licensing and Regulation,* No. 12-0657, 469 S.W.3d 69 (2015).
36. *License to Uber: A Better Way to Fix Irrational Licensing,* 64 UCLA LAW REVIEW ___ (forthcoming 2017).
37. See, e.g., Maria Santos Bier, "Warren and Vitter on 'Too Big to Fail,'" *Cato at Liberty* (blog), September 17, 2015, http://www.cato.org/blog/warren-vitter-too-big-fail.
38. See "Occupational Licensing: A Framework for Policymakers," July 2015, https://www.whitehouse.gov/sites/default/files/docs/licensing_report_final_nonembargo.pdf; "Housing Development Toolkit," September 2016, https://www.whitehouse.gov/sites/whitehouse.gov/files/images/Housing_Development_Toolkit%20f.2.pdf.
39. See, e.g., Derthick and Quirk, *The Politics of Deregulation.*
40. For the origins of this ungainly term for a liberal-libertarian synthesis, see Brink Lindsey, "Liberaltarians," *New Republic,* December 4, 2006, http://www.cato.org/publications/commentary/liberaltarians.
41. John Aldrich and David Rohde, "The Transition to Republican Rule in the House: Implications for Theories of Congressional Government," *Political Science Quarterly* (Winter 1997–98): 541–67.
42. David Dagan and Steven Teles, *Prison Break: Why Conservatives Turned against Mass Incarceration* (New York: Oxford University Press, 2016).
43. Heather Hurlburt and Chayenne Polimedio, "Can Transpartisan Coalitions Overcome Polarization? Lessons from Four Case Studies," New America, April 2016, https://na-production.s3.amazonaws.com/documents/final_transpartisan.pdf.

INDEX